The Gypsies: Their Origin, Continuance, and Destination

Samuel Roberts

THE GYPSIES:

THEIR

ORIGIN, CONTINUANCE, AND DESTINATION,

AS CLEARLY FORETOLD

IN THE

PROPHECIES

OF

ISAIAH, JEREMIAH, AND EZEKIEL,

BY SAMUEL ROBERTS.

"The Prophecies came not by the will of man, but holy men of old spake as they were moved by the Holy Ghost."—2 Peter i., 21.

"Shut up the words and seal the Book even unto the end."—Dan. 12 c., 4 v.

LONDON:

PRINTED FOR

LONGMAN, REES, ORME, BROWN, GREEN, & LONGMAN.

PATERNOSTER-ROW.

1836.

SHEFFIELD :
PRINTED BY WHITAKER AND CO.

CONTENTS.

———

PREFACE.

THE reader of the following work will please to keep constantly in mind that the principal object in view, is to prove, what I think, no one, when he has read it, will venture to deny—that the *Gypsies* are the descendants of the Ancient Egyptians, decreed, by the fiat of the Almighty, as proclaimed by his three great prophets, Isaiah, Jeremiah, and Ezekiel, to be dispersed, for a certain period, in the *wildernesses* and *open fields*, of almost all nations, and to be then gathered to their native land, and taught, under a *Saviour* and a *Great One*, to know the *Lord*. However interesting all else relating to this singular people may be,

B

it is adventitious in respect to the great and
novel truth, which I have undertaken to prove.
It is of no importance, as regards that
fact, whether the people, while in that dispersed state, are respectable or depraved.
If, under such circumstances, they are even
moderately orderly, it must be surprising, and
can only be accounted for, by its being as miraculous an interference as that which decreed
their dispersion, and final restoration. Being
ordained to remain an almost proscribed
people, an alien race, in every land, a certain
degree of orderly conduct was essential to their
being at all tolerated. *That*, I believe, they
will be found generally to have possessed.
But what I wish to impress upon the reader
is, that their conduct, whatever it may be
proved to be, does not affect the *truth*, which
it is my object to establish.

Of the Gypsies, as of all other people,
there, of course, will be found both good and
bad—much may be said for, and much against
them. My own opinion is, that their conduct, on the whole, is so exceedingly superior
to whatever could possibly be expected from
persons, situated as they have been, during so many ages, that nothing less than
Divine controul could have so restrained them.
Surely, it could make nothing against the
miraculous retention of the Jewish people in

their dispersed state, that their conduct was not altogether such as could be wished; neither does it make any thing against it, that some few of them have joined Christian societies; nor does the forsaking of their wandering life by a few of the Gypsies, disprove the fulfilment of the prophecies concerning them; on the contrary, such few and unimportant exceptions only serve to establish the general ordainment the more strongly.

In conclusion, I have only to request the perusal of the following pages, with a mind as free as possible from prejudice, and with a strong desire to be convinced of the *truth*. If that truth prove to be, what I am endeavouring to establish, it is one of the most surprising, interesting, and important discoveries—as regards Divine ordainments—in the general history of mankind, that has been brought to light during the Christian era.

INTRODUCTION.

" Thou hast hid these things from the wise and prudent,
and hast revealed them unto babes."

MATTHEW xi.—25.

ABOUT twenty years ago, Mr. John Hoy-
land, of this town, a member of the Society
of Friends, published a work, entitled
" An Historical Survey of the Customs,
Habits, and Present State of the GYP-
SIES." He, like almost all preceding writers
on the subject, conceived that they were
SOUDRAS, the lowest caste of Hindoos,
driven from their native country by Timour
Beg, in 1408—9.* This work strongly engaged the attention of the author of the following pages; and being then about pub-
lishing a small miscellaneous volume, he in-
serted an article in it, entitled, " *A Word
for the GYPSIES.*" In that he attempted
to prove that they could not possibly be
Soudras, as supposed by Mr. H. and others;
but he was not then able to shew who, or
what, or whence they were. The subject,

---

* It can be proved that the Gypsies were in Europe
before that period.

however, had acquired so much interest in his mind, from the extraordinary nature of the circumstances attending it, that it engrossed much of his subsequent attention. He became at length fully convinced that it was impossible that such a people could be so situated, and so preserved, but, by a miraculous interposition of Almighty power.

The preservation of the Gypsies, as a distinct people, so dispersed in the wilds of all countries, appeared to him as partaking more strongly of the *miraculous* than even that of the JEWS, whose remaining a dispersed people is acknowledged to be by Divine appointment. The idea at length led him to examine if there were any intimations given in the Scriptures, especially in the Prophetic Books, of the preservation of any such people, for he had not then the least recollection of that being the case. His astonishment, therefore, was great indeed, when he found, as he conceived, not only that there was such intimation given, but that there was the most astonishingly clear prediction of *such* a people *so* remaining, that could possibly have been written. More than this, he found such predictions all agreeing with each other, and all applying to such a people, and to no other, in all the three great prophets, viz. Isaiah, Jeremiah, and Ezekiel; not only once in each, but many times recurred to by each of them in the strongest, the most sublime, and yet circumstantial language that inspiration itself could supply. Wonderful as it may seem, no other foretold events have been by any means *so* frequently, *so* strongly, *so* circumstantially repeated, at different times, during the course of a century and a half. These extraordinary discoveries induced him to follow up the subject; and in 1830, he consequently published a small volume, entitled, " Parallel Miracles, or the Jews and the Gypsies." That work having been for some time out of print, his knowledge, his experience, and his views on the subject being now enlarged, and his conviction that his former surmises were correct, as well as that the subject is far more important than he then conceived, he has been induced, in this publication, to enter more fully into the investigation than he before could do.

That predictions such as those alluded to should not have engaged more of the attention of learned scriptural investigators than they have done, does now appear to him to be very extraordinary. No satisfactory explanation has ever yet, so far as he knows, been given of their object; yet that they must have had one, *agreeing with all the predictions in every particular*, every believer in prophecy must, I conceive, admit. " *The Prophecies came not of old times by the will of man, but holy men of God spake as they were moved by the Holy Ghost.*" Now it is utterly impossible to conceive, that one word so spoken, should be either false, superfluous, or in vain. Each had its meaning, and must eventually have its fulfilment. Such prophecies were never wasted on unimportant subjects. They might be, and generally were, conveyed in language which could not be clearly understood till the fulfilment, was at least in the course of taking place,* but *then*, they must be found to agree even in the most minute particulars, so that even the sceptical must be convinced.

Nothing of an earthly nature can be well imagined, more stupendous and important, than that which was the object of these numerous, sublimely awful prophecies. It was no less than the total destruction of the mightest empire that had ever then, that, in many respects, hath ever since, existed. It embraced, not only the total and complete dispersion throughout the world, of all the surviving inhabitants of Egypt, but also of their so remaining a dispersed people during a long period, as well as of their final restoration to

---

* " Shut up the words and seal the book, even to the time of the end."—DANL. xii. 4.

their native country. All these events, too, are foretold to be attended with clearly defined circumstances, as extraordinary in their nature, as they must have then appeared highly improbable, if not totally impossible.

Egypt was then, apparently, like the everlasting mountains, only to be uprooted by the convulsion that should destroy the earth itself. The chosen people of God, had for ages been altogether the most oppressed and abject of Egyptian slaves. They had probably been compelled to erect their temples, to sculpture their idols, and to worship their gods. The fertilizing, wealth-sustaining, plenty-giving *Nile*, almost washed the foundations of the walls of thousands of populous, magnificent palace-containing cities, whose merchants were as princes, and whose monarchs were as gods—asserting, "*my river* (my kingdom) *is mine own, and I have made it myself.*"* Idols and gods were almost as numerous as the people. Such was Egypt! her temples, her palaces, and her tombs, were built or excavated, to defy the tooth of time. They have survived the effects of thousands of years, and if two thousand years more should

---

* While on the commemorative pillars in the countries which they had conquered, was inscribed, " The *King of Kings*, and *Lord of Lords*, subdued this country by his arms."—(See *Herodotus.*)

be to pass before the dispersed people are
to return to their native land, they will, on
arriving there, find many of the temples and
the tombs of their idol-worshipping forefathers, still in existence. The most powerful, the most magnificent, and the wisest of
all the monarchs of God's favoured people
himself, solicited, and obtained, the daughter
of her king to share with him the throne
of the heaven-favoured race of Abraham.
Egypt was acknowledged, not only to have
been the fountain, but also the reservoir of
all the then existing arts and sciences.

Such was EGYPT, when, by the command of the Almighty, three of his prophets,
at different periods, and in numerous instances, predicted her speedy and total overthrow. They did more than this; they predicted the complete dispersion of her people,
not in their own or neighbouring countries,
but in distant countries of the north, the very
names and existence of some of which were
then unknown to them. Through these were
the most numerous, powerful, magnificent
people on the face of the earth decreed to be
scattered, and neither to be brought together
nor *gathered*. They were to be houseless
wandering vagabonds; they were to be thrown
into the *wildernesses*; they were to fall upon
the *open fields*. Surely these would have

been wonderful predictions respecting any people at any time. They were, however, only the beginning of wonders. These dwellers in marble palaces, these builders of gorgeous temples, these excavators of magnificent everlasting tombs, were to become *despised* among the most *despicable*. *Their bodies were to be given for meat to the beasts of the field and to the fowls of the heavens.* These god-manufacturers, these worshippers of idols (living and dead) innumerable, it was boldly declared by the prophets, should, in their dispersed state, be totally *without IDOLS.*

Such are the extraordinary predictions, it may be said, of God himself, for they are ushered in by " *Thus saith the Lord God !*" In this extraordinary, unexampled state, spread or scattered in the *wildernesses*, in the *open fields* of all countries, they were decreed to remain, and to be preserved a distinct people, during *forty years*—they are then (for I conclude that the forty years cannot be *yet* expired) to be gathered from among all the people whither they have been scattered, to the land of their fathers, and are there, though a base kingdom, to be *taught to know the Lord.*

The foregoing, it must be acknowledged, are the most extraordinary predictions that ever issued respecting any people from the mouths of the inspired *holy men of old!* The circumstances are so numerous, so singular, and so clear, that they never could apply to *two* races of human beings: yet, in this case, they must apply to one in *every particular.* We believe that the dispersed Egyptians never *have* returned to their native land, and *known the Lord,* nor had, as predicted, " *a Saviour and a Great One."* If so, and if there be one word of truth in any prophecies, they must be existing at this time in their dispersed state; and must, when the fulness of time is come, return to the land of their forefathers, and there become a *Christian people.*

Where then, it may be asked, are those extraordinary people, on whose existence the truth of prophecy and the accuracy of the Scriptures depend? If they exist at all, they cannot be hid, for they are to be in all countries; they cannot be mistaken, since their peculiarities are so numerous and so striking. Ask not, then, *where* the scattered Egyptians are, but rather ask *where they are not?* What country has not heard of them? for few countries are without them.

During four or five hundred years, they have been *known* to have been occupying the *wildernesses* and the *open fields* of almost every country in Europe. They have from the first told every one *who* they were and *whence they came.* Though they knew nothing about Egypt, they *all, always,* asserted that they were EGYPTIANS. Nobody believed them, because, as predicted, they were *despised.* Images and idols they have none ; they *have ceased.* They have, as a people, no religion. In all countries they are in all respects the same ; all speaking the same language. Now, then, *if the* GYPSIES *are not the dispersed Egyptians, what are they? If the dispersed and scattered Gypsies are not the descendants of the offending Egyptians, where are that scattered people?*

If any enlightened individual were required to describe a people, who in every respect would answer to the Egyptians in the state denounced against them, by all the three major prophets, it were impossible for that person to describe such a people more clearly, and fully agreeing with the extraordinary denouncements, than the *Gypsies* now do, and have done, at all times, ever since they have been publicly noticed, and described at all. Without a miraculous interference, no people could be preserved in such a state ; to the Egyptians and to the Jews *only,* have such an interference ever been promised. That the Gypsies could not be Soudras, will, in the course of

the present work, be fully proved. Indeed,
the only tenable ground for such a supposition, is, that there are many words in the
languages spoken by each people very similar
in sound. Now there are many reasons for
believing that both languages sprung from
the same root, but that they had, from time,
and circumstances, become, in a great measure,
distinct languages, the existing degree of
similarity then, serves to *confirm* the supposition, that the Gypsies are the descendants
of the ancient Egyptians. The following
quotation from the History of Egypt, in the
Edinburgh Cabinet Library, may serve to
corroborate that opinion:—

" It has long been an object of inquiry
among scholars to discover the channel
through which civilization, science, and an
acquaintance with the liberal arts, first reached the valley which is watered by the Nile.
Without analyzing the numerous hypotheses
which have been successively formed and
abandoned, or repeating the various conjectures which have, age after age, amused the
ingenuity of the learned, we shall state at
once, as the most probable of the opinions
entertained on this subject, that the stream
of knowledge accompanied the progress of
commerce along the banks of those great
rivers which fall into the Persian Gulf, and

thence along the coast of Arabia to the shores of the Red Sea. There is the best reason to believe that those passes or lateral defiles, which connect the sea just named, with the river of Egypt, witnessed the earliest migration of colonists from Asia; who, in the pursuits of commerce, or in search of more fertile lands, or of mountains enriched with gold, found their way into Nubia and Abyssinia. Meantime, it is probable, a similar current set eastward across the mouths of the Indus, carrying arts and institutions of a corresponding character into the countries which stretch from that river to the great peninsula of Indostan.

"The most obvious confirmation of the opinion now stated, may be drawn from the striking resemblance which is known to subsist between the usages, the superstitions, the arts, and the mythology of the ancient inhabitants of Western India, and those of the first settlers on the Upper Nile. The temples of Nubia, for example, exhibit the same features, whether as to the style of architecture, or the form of worship to which they were devoted, with the similiar buildings which have been recently examined in the neighbourhood of Bombay. In both cases they consist of vast excavations hewn out in the solid body of a hill or mountain, and are decorated with huge figures which indicate the same powers of nature, or serve as emblems to denote the same qualities in the ruling spirits of the universe.

"As a further proof of this hypothesis, we are informed that the sepoys who joined the British army in Egypt, under Lord Hutchinson, imagined that they found their own temples in the ruins of Dendera, and were greatly exasperated at the natives for their neglect of the ancient deities, whose images are still preserved. So strongly, indeed, were they impressed with this identity, that they proceeded to perform their devotions with all the ceremonies practised in their own land."

Every thing, then, seems to prove, that the Gypsies of the present day, are the reserved scattered people, whose dispersion, continuance, and return to Egypt, the three prophets, by the express command of the Almighty, foretold so frequently, so strongly, and so explicitly, through a period of a century and a half.

If we look back upon the wonderful occurrences of the last half century, as they relate to the general acquisition of knowledge respecting Egypt, and as to their contributing to compel intense attention to that, before comparatively little known, country;—the conviction can hardly fail to follow, that God is preparing the world by those events, for disclosures and circumstances connected with that first and most wonderful nation and people, such as have never yet been anticipated. It is possible, and even probable, that this *more than assumption* of the Gypsies being the descendants of the ancient Egyptians, may prove to be one of the appointed means for producing such fore-ordained occurrences.

The great difficulty will be in inducing the public to entertain the subject seriously at all. The people implicated are, in their estimation, too insignificant, worthless, and vile, to merit any appropriation of either their time or notice—a race of annoying, houseless vagabonds, impostors, deceiving and cheating wherever they can, being so conscious of their guilt, that they always endeavour to avoid society.

Now, if these people were not this homeless, wandering, despised race, they could not possibly be the people which, it is the object of this publication, to prove that they are: whatever their conduct, as to honesty, may be, it does not at all affect their claim to being the descendants of the ancient Egyptians. In that respect, however, it will be shown, that they have been much more sinned against, than sinning. It would, indeed, seem almost impossible to conceive of a people *so* situated, whose conduct could have been so little reprehensible. Their present abject state, contrasted with that of their supposed forefathers, at the time when the prophets of the Lord, so minutely foretold their present degradation, adds greatly to the interest of the subject.

The Gypsies certainly are not more opposed in either sentiments or conduct, to the purity of Christianity, than are their supposed fellow-sufferers from the indignation of an offended God, the JEWS. How astonishingly does it add to the sublimity, the awfulness, and the importance of the subject, when it is conceived, that the two people have, during thousands of years, been linked together in advancement, in transgressions, in threatenings, in predictions, in prosperity, in extirpation, in being driven from their native land, as outcast wanderers over the face of the whole world. The one people in the cities hoarding up wealth, and the others in the *open fields*, houseless and penny-less, each being to this day constantly striking, convincing, mementos of the truth of prophecy, of hatred, of sin, and of the sure vengeance of a disregarded and insulted God, to all the people and nations on the face of the earth. Consider them in this light, and they are neither to be despised as unworthy of notice, nor to be disregarded as prognosticators of the sure fulfilment of the remaining part of the awfully important prophetic denunciations.

Who can read the following prediction of the prophet Isaiah against the two people, the Jews and the Egyptians, without feeling a conviction that their lot is cast *together?* " When the Lord shall stretch out his hand, both he that *helpeth* shall fall, and he that is *helpen* shall fall down, and *they shall fail TOGETHER."* Together they rose, together they fell; and if there be truth in the sure word of prophecy, they will together be raised up, together restored to their native lands, together be brought to know the Lord, who shall send them a SAVIOUR and a GREAT ONE. In all human probability the conversion of the Gypsies to Christianity will clearly be as entirely the work of Almighty power, as their conquest, dispersion, and preservation as a distinct people have been. This, though a discouragement, ought not to paralize the efforts of pious Christians to bring some of them to a knowledge of the truth as it is in Christ Jesus our Lord. The obstacles are by no means so great as in the case of the Jews. The Gypsies are much more willing to listen to Christian teachers. They have stronger feelings, are more easily wrought upon, and have much fewer old established prejudices to overcome. Still the impression made on the Gypsies will rarely be lasting, and they will generally avoid a repetition of those feelings of which the ridicule of the rest of their people will too often make them ashamed. Let not, however, the Christian teacher despair, God only can give the increase.

PARALLEL MIRACLES, &c.

THE ANCIENT EGYPTIANS.

> " After these appear'd
> A crew, who, under names of old renown,
> Osiris, Isis, Orus, and their train,
> With monstrous shapes and sorceries, abused
> Fanatic Egypt and her priests, to seek
> Their wandering gods, disguised in brutish forms
> Rather than human. Nor did Israel 'scape
> The infection, when their borrow'd gold composed
> The calf in Oreb; and the rebel-king
> Doubled that sin in Bethel and in Dan,
> Likening his Maker to the grazed ox,—
> Jehovah, who in one night, when He pass'd,
> From Egypt marching, equall'd with one stroke
> Both her first-born and all her bleating gods."
> PARADISE LOST, BOOK I.

IT is one of the most exalted and interesting exercises of the human faculties to contemplate, at this distance of time, the rise, the progress, the splendour, the declension, and the extinction of the more renowned among the nations of remote antiquity.

This is particularly the case, when numerous, massive, and stupendous evidences of the existence, and the powerful magnificence of such nations still remain, after having survived the destructive efforts of time, of barbarism, and of the elements, through thousands of years.

The pleasure and utility of the contemplation are increased, when the history of the now extinct nation is evidently and intimately connected with the progress of that Divine government of the universe which is always the same, and with which we are, as they were, connected and interested; and still more so, when that nation seems clearly to have been one of the first links in an unbroken chain, which we can trace from the creation through all successive ages, to our own days; a chain with which we are connected, and which we can view by the eye of faith, illumined by the light of prophecy, extending forward into distant futurity even to the end of time. This interest is still further augmented when the history is one which seized upon our attention as soon as the opening faculties of the mind began to unfold; the events recorded being of a nature calculated irresistibly to imprint themselves. in characters not to be obliterated, on the unoccupied tablet of the youthful mind. Such is the history of the ancient Egyptians.

The Egyptian appears to have been one of the first, if not the very first, of the powerful kingdoms that were formed in the postdiluvian world. Within four hundred years after the flood, we find Abram, one of the early descendants of Noah, with his

family, (himself being " very rich in silver, and in
gold") seeking refuge from famine with the King
and the Princes of Egypt.

Again, the history of Joseph is one which no
child ever read without being highly delighted, nor
without remembering it while memory survived.
Egypt is, as the scene of most of his wonderful ad-
ventures, too intimately combined with the history,
not to be always afterwards associated with the
recollection of it.

When, at length, (which is the next important
step with which we are acquainted in the history of
that country) " there arose up a new King over
Egypt, which knew not Joseph," a series of events
occur of so astonishing a nature, that the mind of
youth rarely fails to recur to them with constantly
renewed interest. They have all the overpowering
effects of the wildest romance, added to the full
force of the simplest truth.

The Egyptians appear to afford the most striking example with which we are acquainted of the
utter weakness of all mere human strength when
opposed to the power of the Almighty. If they
ever possessed any knowledge of the true God, they
seem very soon utterly to have disregarded and despised it. Their strength, though great, was the
strength of man, and their wisdom, though extensive, was the wisdom of man. They were the declared oppressors of God's people, and the open
determined opposers of the Divine will and word.
God seems to have suffered them to attain all that
human faculties could acquire, that they might be

his instruments in the chastisement of his stubborn and rebellious children ; and then, (after existing sixteen hundred years) when they had so far answered his purpose, his power was made manifest in their overthrow, and the stupendous ruins of their magnificence and greatness decreed to be reserved probably to the end of time, as a lasting and memorable lesson to future generations ; teaching them the vanity and nothingness of all mere mortal efforts.

The human eye, and mind, cannot contemplate the ruins of the works of this astonishing people, as they exist at this remote period of time, without the utmost admiration. They are of such stupendous magnitude as to compel the notice of the most inattentive observer, they seem as if formed for the purpose of rendering the lesson which they were intended to teach not only impressive, but everlasting and universal. The attention of the whole world, too, has, in an extraordinary manner been drawn to them by recent events, as wonderful in their nature as the objects themselves are. No other works of man, in any part of the world, can bear a comparison with the ruins of Egypt. Bulk and magnitude with durability, having been the ends aimed at, they certainly do, in those respects, set all former and subsequent attempts at defiance. We are told of the united efforts of two thousand men, constantly applied during two years, in the removal of one single stone from the place where it was got, to that which it was intended to occupy. Almost all their palaces, their temples, and their tombs, partook in a great measure, of the same magnificent durable character.

The learning and the wisdom of the Egyptians appear to have astonished the people of that generation, as much as their buildings and other stupendous works. To be "learned in all the wisdom of the Egyptians," was the greatest encomium that could be passed on the acquirements of Moses; and the highest character that could be given to the wisdom of the wisest of mortals, was, that "it exceeded the wisdom of all the East country, and all the wisdom of Egypt."

Of all the nations of the earth, the Egyptians were the most addicted to idolatry and superstitious observances. In no country whatever, did the influence of the priests and magicians, extend so universally and so unboundedly as in Egypt. It was the very cradle of polytheism. The heavens, the earth, the air, and the water, abounded with the false gods which they were taught to worship; and, as if all these combined, were insufficient to afford them deities in the requisite numbers, they made such for themselves, of stocks and stones, of wood and metal of every kind. Every house, nay almost every individual, had gods of their own.

The wealth of all the land was at the command of the priests, for the bodies of the highest nobles, nay of their kings themselves, could not receive those rites of interment which were declared to be essential to future blessedness, but by the consent of the priests. Accordingly we find, that the most massive and magnificent of all their structures, were those erected for the worship of idols, or for the entombment of the dead. As if determined to counteract the course of nature, and the decree of the Almighty, they sought to render even their perishable bodies immortal. The sums lavished on this most hopeless attempt, and absurd folly, were beyond all conception great. To our own days, through more than three thousand years, have many of these painted sepulchral envelopes, these preserved memorials of disgusting mortality, come down. These costly noble, perhaps royal carcases, are now distributed over all the civilized world, as mementos of the vanity of all attempts to perpetuate human distinction. Scarcely the name of any one of them is known, and the sight of the noblest of them all, is horrible and disgusting.

By this idolatrous nation the chosen people of God were tempted to sin, whenever they came (which was frequently the case) in contact with them. Such a people as this, could not be expected to escape the just vengeance of the Almighty when the measure of their iniquity was full, and when they had accomplished the purposes of Omniscience, for which they had till then been permitted to exist as a distinct race. With God the wisest and the mightiest are as easily discomfited and overthrown as the most ignorant and weak. Accordingly the command of the Most High was given, and their degradation, their sufferings, and their abjectness, became as conspicuous as their grandeur, their pride, and their greatness had before been.

It cannot be either a useless or unprofitable

employment of time and reason, to examine at some
length, and with attention, these important events
connected with their probable consequences. The
the awful and tremendous lesson which God had
previously taught to mankind by the extirpation of
almost all the human race at the flood, appears to
have made very little beneficial impression on these
infatuated people. They were, it is probable, to
the full as wicked as most of those who perished
with the old world.

When, then, God *was* aroused to take vengeance
on such an ungrateful and rebellious people, it
might be expected that the judgments would be as
signal as exemplary. Accordingly we find that
this awful event was ushered in with peculiarly impressive circumstances. The greatest prophets of
his chosen race were selected and commissioned to
proclaim its approach in the clearest, the most forcible, and the most alarming denunciations that prophetic language itself could furnish.

The circumstances which immediately led to
these denunciations, and the subsequent overthrow,
captivity, and dispersion of the Egyptians are the
following :—

A remnant of Judah was left by Nebuchadnezzar
in the land of their forefathers after he had sacked
Jerusalem, destroyed the temple, and carried away
the treasures thereof, with almost all the people,
captive to Babylon. This remnant, distrusting the
power and the goodness of the Lord their God, determined, in spite of the earnest solicitations and
loud threatenings of the prophet Jeremiah, to flee

for safety to the idolatrous Egyptians. " Be not afraid of the King of Babylon," said the prophet ; " of whom ye are afraid ; be not afraid of *him*, saith the Lord ; for I am with you to save you, and to deliver you out of his hand ; and I will show mercies unto you, and cause you to return to your own land.   But if ye say, we will not dwell in this land, neither obey the voice of the Lord our God, saying, No ! but we will go into the land of Egypt, where we shall see no more war, nor hear the sound of the trumpet, nor have hunger of bread ; and there will we dwell :—And now, therefore, hear the voice of the Lord, ye remnant of Judah ; thus saith the Lord of hosts, the God of Israel ; if ye wholly set your faces to go into Egypt, and go to sojourn there ; then it shall come to pass, that the sword which ye feared shall overtake you there in the land of Egypt ; and there ye shall die," Jeremiah, xlii.

This was not the first time, by many, that God had by the mouth of his prophets forbidden the Israelites to flee for succour to the idolatrous Egyptians.   The prophet Isaiah had long before denounced a woe upon them if they did so. " Woe to them that go down to Egypt for help, and stay on horses and trust in chariots, because they are many ; but they look not to the Holy One of Israel, nor seek the Lord. * * * The Egyptians are men and not God ; and their horses flesh and not spirit ; when the Lord shall stretch out his hand, both he that helpeth shall fall, and he that is helpen shall fall down, and they shall fail together," Isaiah,

xxxi. 1 and 3. Notwithstanding these repeated warnings and denunciations, and in spite of all former fatal experiences, the blind and infatuated Israelites threw themselves for protection into the arms of the deadliest of their enemies, by whom they were again induced to forsake the worship of the true God for that of beasts, and stocks, and stones,—probably, too, of man, for it is intimated of Pharaoh Hophra, the then King of Egypt, that it was not in the power of the gods themselves to dethrone him, "for," said he, "my river is mine own, and I have made it for myself."

The measure of the iniquity of the Egyptians, and the obstinate wickedness and folly of the people of Israel, were now nearly full. It therefore became time for the Lord to lay bare his red right arm to take signal vengeance on them both, and to appoint them to be perpetual memorials of his power and justice to every nation on the face of the earth, to the remotest period of time. The Egyptians, as the primal transgressors, and as the tempters, were the first to suffer. The punishment of the Jews was not long delayed ; but with this we have not at present farther to do in this part of the work, than as in connexion with that of the Egyptians.

Never was any Judgment of God ushered in with such grand, such awful, such frequently repeated denunciations as this of the Egyptians. Never was any future event more clearly and more strikingly foretold. Isaiah, Ezekiel, and Jeremiah, each predict their marvellous overthrow and subse-

quent dispersion among the other nations, with a
minuteness and frequency not equalled, I believe,
on any other occasion. With what awful sublimity
doth Ezekiel declare (chap. 29) in the figurative
language of the east, and in the name of God,
" Behold I am against thee, Pharaoh, King, of Egypt,
the great dragon that lieth in the midst of his rivers,
which hath said, my river is mine own, and I have
made it for myself. But I will put hooks in thy
jaws. I will cause the fish of thy rivers to stick
unto thy scales, and I will bring thee up out of the
midst of thy rivers, and all the fish of thy rivers
shall stick unto thy scales. And I will leave thee
thrown into the *wilderness*, thee and all the fish of
thy rivers ; *thou shalt fall upon* OPEN FIELDS ; *thou
shalt not be brought together nor gathered :* I have
given thee for meat to the beasts of the field, and
to the fowls of the heaven. And all the inhabitants of Egypt shall know that I am the Lord, because they have been a staff of reed to the house of
Israel. When they took hold of thee by thy hand
thou didst break, and rend all their shoulders : and
when they leaned upon thee, thou brakest, and
madest all their loins to be at a stand." Again, in
still plainer language, in the same chapter, " Behold,
therefore, I am against thee, and against thy rivers,
and I will make the land of Egypt utterly waste
and desolate from the tower of Syene, even unto
the borders of Ethiopia. No foot of man shall pass
through it, nor foot of beast shall pass through it,
neither shall it be inhabited forty years. And I
will make the land of Egypt desolate among the

countries that are desolate, and her cities among
the cities that are laid waste shall be desolate forty
years : and I will scatter the Egyptians among the
nations, and will disperse them through the countries. Yet saith the Lord God, *at the end of forty
years*, I will gather the Egyptians from among the
people whither they are scattered ; and I will bring
again the captivity of Egypt, and will cause them
to return unto the land of Pathros, into the land of
their habitation, and they shall be there a base
kingdom."

In the thirtieth chapter the prophet saith—
" Thus saith the Lord God ; I will destroy the
Idols, and will cause their images to cease out of
Noph ; and there shall be no more princes of the
land of Egypt : and I will put a fear in the land of
Egypt." Isaiah, in the nineteenth chapter, after
foretelling the evils that should come upon Egypt,
speaking of subsequent events, declares, that " In
that day there shall be an altar to the Lord in the
midst of Egypt, and a pillar at the border thereof
to the Lord. And it shall be for a sign and for a
witness unto the Lord of Hosts in the land of
Egypt ; for they shall cry unto the Lord because
of the oppressors, and He shall send them a Saviour,
and a Great One, and He shall deliver them. And
the Lord shall be known to Egypt, and the Egyptians shall know the Lord in that day, and shall
do sacrifice and oblations, yea they shall vow a
vow unto the Lord, and shall perform it. And the
Lord shall smite Egypt, He shall smite it and
heal it : and they shall return even unto the Lord,

and he shall be entreated of them, and shall heal
them."

These prophecies are repeated, particularly by
Ezekiel, many times almost in the same words in
different chapters (see particularly the whole of the
30th and 32d,) as if he were desirous in an especial
manner to enforce them. These denunciations and
prophecies, then, seem clearly to establish three
distinct important events to the Egyptians. First,
their complete conquest and dispersion; secondly,
their remaining dispersed, *without idols*, among all
nations and countries, *in the open fields*, during
forty years; and finally their being again brought
to the land of their habitation, where they shall be
taught to know the Lord.

It remains, in the next place, to consider what
part of these numerous prophecies have been already fulfilled, and what parts, if any, still remain
to be completed.

The conquest of Egypt by Nebuchadnezzar, took
place soon after the prophesying of Ezekiel, but
Egypt did not cease to be a kingdom, though a
tributary one, till more than forty years afterwards,
when it became a province of other kingdoms, and
has so remained ever since: first to the Persians,
then to the Macedonians, the Romans, the Saracens,
the Mamelukes, and lastly to the Turks. Hitherto,
then, it is clearly evident that the prophecies cannot all have been fulfilled. The prediction of forty
years' dispersion " among all nations and countries
whither the Lord had driven them," could not refer to
the forty years subsequent to the conquest of Egypt.

by Nebuchadnezzar : in that period no such events as there predicted took place ; on the contrary, it was not till after then that Egypt entirely ceased to be a kingdom ; that their idols were destroyed, and that their images ceased out of Noph. Then, however, they did cease to be a people. They were gone, and no one knew whither ; for they were "dispersed among the nations and scattered through the countries." To this day they have never returned ! Their language has been long forgotten in the land of their habitation, and their temples, their palaces, and their tombs, are despised, defiled, or destroyed.

Whenever any particular specific period for the fulfilment of any prophecy is mentioned in Scripture, I believe that is always a longer period prefigured by a shorter one. This is clearly the case in those of Daniel ; nor is the exact period prefigured, always understood before the final accomplishment of the prophecy. In the present instance then, the forty years, during which the Egyptians were to remain "scattered among the countries of the uncircumcised," most certainly typifies a much longer period.* Whatever the period may be, it is evident that it is not yet expired, since no such events as those then predicted to take place have occurred.

Where, then, it will be enquired, have been, and still are, the Egyptians so dispersed, *in the open fields*, among all nations? This is a question which

* May it not in this instance mean forty Jubilee years, or two thousand from some epoch ?

it will be a principal object of the remaing pages
of this work to answer.   It is a question that involves much more than the gratification of mere
curiosity ; the truth of Scripture history, the fulfilment of prophecies ; the accounting for great difficulties, and intensely interesting circumstances,
in the history of one of the most singular people
known on the face of the earth, as well as the promotion of the future welfare, both temporal and
eternal, of that people, are involved in the answer
to that important question.

In proceeding then to that reply, I would do it
with all due consideration and seriousness ; humbly
trusting that if I should not be able fully to clear
up the mystery, I may in some degree, lessen the
obscurity that has hitherto hung over it, or at least
arouse curiosity, and thereby induce abler investigators to prosecute more successful efforts.

THE GYPSIES.

———

"I see a column of slow-rising smoke
O'ertop the lofty wood, that skirts the wild.
A wandering and houseless tribe there eat
Their miserable meal.   A kettle, slung
Between two poles, upon a stick transverse,
Receives the morsel.   *   *   *
*   *   *   Hard faring race !
Their scanty fuel from the neighbouring wood,
When kindled with dry leaves, just saves unquench'd
The spark of life.   The sportive wind blows wide
Their fluttering rags, and shews a tawny skin,
The vellum of the pedigree they claim."

———

During many centuries, a people have been known
to exist in almost every country in Europe, and in
some of those of Asia, of very peculiar appearance,
manners, and habits ; speaking a language unknown
to all of them.   It is now more than four hundred
years since the first notice of them, that is come down
to us, was taken.   They then existed in perhaps all
the countries in which they are now found, and from
their acquaintance at that time with the languages,
prejudices, and customs of the several countries in
which they resided, it is evident that they must have

been resident in them long before that time. Why no particular account of them, written before then, has reached us, may be easily explained. Their habits were always such, that there rarely resided more than a few families together; they shunned large towns, they were continually removing from place to place, and dispersed as they were, *in the open fields*, in all countries, their numbers in each did not appear considerable. Before that period, the wild and uncultivated parts of every country in Europe, were so great and numerous, that an inoffensive unobtrusive people, so dispersed, might remain for ages little known or noticed. Before the invention of printing, any written notice taken of them by individuals, would be little read, and soon neglected or forgotten. If, then, this singular people had resided in all the countries, as they do now, for twenty centuries befor the time mentioned, it is possible that no previous notice of them might have reached us. The probability is, that they had been long so dispersed, little molesting others, and being but little molested themselves.

Whence this singular people came, why they came, and how they came, are questions which seem hitherto to have proved very perplexing or very unaccountably disregarded. To endeavour, then, to answer all these curious questions, cannot but be an interesting, and it may be a useful investigation. To this day, they seem to have continued from the time we have the first account of them unchanged in any respect; and perhaps with but little variation in their numbers. No European

nation is free from them, nor is any one overstocked
with them.   With every people among whom they
reside, they in many respects assimilate, but with
none do they incorporate. By most nations during
the last four hundred years, they have, more or less,
been persecuted ; yet in no instance have they been
driven away or extirpated.   In no country have
they ever made the least attempt to obtain supre-
macy, landed property, or even rank of any kind,
yet in none have they ever been reduced to bond-
age ; seldom to servitude.   They can speak the
language of every country in which they reside,
but in no instance have they been known to substitute it to the exclusion of their own.   In countries possessing them all, *they* have no temples, no
palaces, no tombs, nor any buildings whatever.
They have no learning, no teachers, no scholars, no
books, no letters. They have no religion, no priests,
no gods, no idols, no images.   Possessing no peculiar customs or privileges, to keep them a distinct
people, they still remain so from age to age, in all
climes, amidst all nations, and under all circumstances.   This is the more remarkable, as they conform, without opposition, seemingly without objection, to the peculiarities, both civil and religious, of
all the people in whose countries they reside.   In
wars they have never willingly been concerned.
They are contented with the scantiest measure of
food, and the simplest and plainest aliment, suffices
to satisfy them.   They affect no peculiarity of
dress, ornament, or method of wearing their hair or
beard ; but, in these respects, conform in a great

measure to the practices of the countries in which
they reside, at least so far as to avoid ridicule or
peculiar notice. In fixed trades or professions, they
never or rarely engage ; yet they are not idle, but,
whenever opportunity offers, pursue such trades,
as are capable of being carried on with their itinerant life and habits.

These are some of the peculiar circumstances attached to that most extraordinary race, the Gypsies,
" dispersed through all the kingdoms, and scattered
throughout all countries." The dispersion and continuance, as a distinct people, of the Jews through
so many ages, is considered as clearly miraculous :
and would be so considered, even setting prophecy
apart ; but the dispersion and continuance of the
Gypsies, a distinct people, through so many ages in
all countries, is beyond measure *more* astonishing.
The Jews abound with peculiarities, both civil and
religious, which preclude *their* assimilating with
any other people. The Gypsies possess no such
peculiarities, and yet they continue equally detached from all others. Surely, then, it is clearly
evident that the state of the Gypsies is, at least,
equally miraculous with that of the Jews ; and we
have good ground to warrant us in looking for evidence to establish the supposition.

In the first place, then, whence came the Gypsies?
Their name as a people, and their own oral testimony in all countries, establish beyond all reasonable doubt, *that they are EGYPTIANS.* They have
never, in any country, or any period of time, given
any other account of themselves. It is utterly im-

possible, that such a belief and testimony should so universally prevail among the whole of a people so dispersed, with no communication whatever from age to age with each other, and who, on any other supposition, could know nothing of Egypt, if it were not true. It is impossible that this could be true of the Gypsies if it were not *miraculous*. In tracing, then, their origin, it is necessary to search for evidence to support the claim to miraculous interference.

An attempt has already been made to give a slight sketch of the ancient Egyptians, and their history ;—thence it appears, that they had often grievously offended the Almighty, but more especially in the end, by their gross idolatry, by their king having declared himself to be God ; and by their having induced the Israelites to trust in *their* strength, rather than in that of the Lord of Hosts : God, therefore, denounced great and awful judgments against them by no less than three of his prophets. Sufficient of those denunciations have been here brought forward to shew the purport and tendency of them. Those prophecies and denunciations have hitherto been only in part accomplished ; the remainder of them relate to a people who have not been heard of, scarcely thought of, during more than two thousand years, yet they must exist *somewhere*, or the prophecies cannot be fulfilled. The singularity of their situation, as then declared, is such that, when found, they scarcely can be mistaken for any others.

After a lapse of nearly two thousand years, a

people were discovered, or then first brought forward into public notice, which, in every circumstance relating to them, seem to resemble the people so lost ; and they are so circumstanced, that if
they are not that people, it seems utterly impossible
to account for the peculiarity of their situation and
habits, or to say who they are. *If the Gypsies*
are not the dispersed Egyptians, where are that
scattered people ?   If the dispersed and scattered
Gypsies are not the descendants of the offending
Egyptians, what are they ? The ancient language
of the Egyptians is a lost language ; the language
of the Gypsies is one that is spoken by no other
people, and yet it is universally the same with
them in every nation and in every country throughout the world in which they are scattered.

There is one very peculiar circumstance respecting the Gypsies. Though they profess, as a people, no purer religion, yet they worship no *idols ;*
they have no *images* among them. This, at first
sight, would seem to militate against their being
from Egypt, the very nursery of polytheism ; but
farther reflection will prove it to be a strong confirmation of their being the dispersed Egyptians.
On any other supposition, it is impossible to account for so singular a circumstance.

Respecting the offending Egyptians, God declared, by the mouth of his prophet, " I will destroy their *idols*, and I will cause their *images* to
cease." Here, then, is a sufficient cause to produce such an effect, and the only cause apparently
capable of producing it ; God being expressly de-

clared to have ordained it in this one instance, and
in this one instance only. No other people so circumstanced were ever known to have been without
objects of worship. God's depriving the Egyptians
of these idolatrous objects, is, in what appears
to be his usual course of dispensing his judgments, viz., depriving the transgressors of those
things by which they sinned, or by which they
were led to transgress.

This is not the only instance in which the hand
of God is thus made visible in their case, on the
supposition that the Gypsies are the ancient Egpy-
tians: for instance, the Egyptians prided themselves
most particularly on the magnitude and durability
of their structures, whether palaces, temples, or
tombs. The Gypsies have not any of these. A
slight, moveable, perishable covering of cloth, serves
them to be born, to live, and to die in. The Egyptians regarded themselves, and were regarded by
others, as the wisest and most learned people on
the face of the earth ; looking down with contempt
on all other. Few of the Gypsies, even in countries where the poorest are learned, (Scotland,)
know a letter ; nor was there ever as far as I know,
a single sentence written in their language since
their dispersion. The Egyptians were luxurious
in their eating, beyond most, if not all the nations
of antiquity. The Gypsies subsist on the plainest
food, even the carcases of dead animals that are
thrown out or left to rot. The Egyptians were
splendid in their attire, vain of their dress, and of
their great riches. The Gypsies are generally

clothed in rags, abjectly poor, and despised by the
vilest of the meanest people. The dead bodies of
the Egyptians were preserved at an expense, and
deposited in splendour, such as the world never
witnessed on such occasions, either before or since
their time.* The dead bodies of the Gypsies are
disposed of without either expense or ceremonies ;
the grave of a Gipsy is scarcely known in the
world. " They shall be desolate amidst the countries that are desolate," said the Lord ; and there
is no people in the civilized world so desolate, that

* The following is the interesting relation of the death,
the embalming, and the burying of Jacob, as given in the
50th chapter of Genesis :—

" And when Jacob had made an end of commanding
his sons, he gathered up his feet into the bed, and yielded
up the ghost, and was gathered unto his people. And
Joseph fell upon his father's face, and wept upon him,
and kissed him.

" And Joseph commanded his servants, the physicians,
to embalm his father ; and the physicians embalmed Israel.
And forty days were fulfilled for him : for so are fulfilled
the days of those who are embalmed : and the Egyptians
mourned for him three-score and ten days.

    *   *   *   *   *

" And Joseph went up to bury his father ; and with
him went up all the servants of Pharaoh, the elders of
his house, and all the elders of the land of Egypt ; and
all the house of Joseph, and his brethren and his father's
house.

" And there went up with him both chariots and horse-
men, and it was a very great company. And they came
to the threshing floor at Atad, which is beyond Jordan ;
and there they mourned with a very great and sore
lamentation : and he made a mourning for his father
seven days."

the Gypsies would not appear among them more so. This *must* be the Lord's doing, it is indeed marvellous in our eyes!

If we believe in the miraculous dispersion, and future recal to their own country, of the Jews, I do not see how we can withhold our assent to the scattering among all countries, and subsequent re-assembling in " the land of their habitation" of the Egyptians. Both occurrences are declared by the same prophets; the latter fully as frequently, as strongly, and as plainly as the former. The two events are so intimately connected, that it seems scarcely possible to separate them ; and they mutually add confirmation, interest, and importance to each other. " When the Lord shall stretch out his hand," saith the prophet Isaiah, speaking of the Jews and the Egyptians, "both he that helpeth, and he that is helpen, shall fall down, and they shall fail together." It is probable that the number of the scattered Egyptians may not be very inferior to that of the dispersed Jews, and it is not impossible that the former may be the pioneers appointed to clear the way for the returning Israelites, (the fulness of the Gentiles being first to come in,) as they were the instruments of their dispersion. The conversion of the Egyptians may indeed be the instrument appointed for the conversion of the Jews. In conjunction, the two events increase the awful solemnity of the Jewish re-assemblage in the land of Judah most exceedingly. The future temporal state of the two people, however, appears to be intended to be very different. The Egyptians are, it is said, to be an abject nation; but as they are finally to be taught to know the Lord, to be healed, and to have a Saviour, their dispersion and sufferings will not have been to them in vain.

As very erroneous ideas of the present state and manners of the Gypsies are pretty generally entertained, it may not be improper or useless to endeavour, in this place, as far as truth will warrant, to lessen the prejudices which exist against them. Though they have almost always been considered and described as rogues and vagabonds, and have generally been treated in all countries as such, the imputation rarely seems to rest upon proof. On the contrary, they who have so described them, have mostly admitted that they have taken their character on hearsay; while those who have had opportunities of *really* knowing them, have generally affirmed that they have not found them to be such.

Pasquier, in his " Recherches de la France," gives an account of their appearing in considerable numbers in that country in the year 1427, copied from an old book written by a Doctor of Divinity i n Paris. The description in many respects seems correct; but the accounts which he says they gave of themselves, if they were Gypsies, were evidently meant to deceive those of whom they were afraid. He says, " they were the poorest and most miserable looking people that had ever been seen in France; yet notwithstanding their poverty, and seeming ignorance, they had women among them, who, by looking into people's hands, told their fortunes. And what was worse, they picked people's pockets of their money, and got it into their own, through telling these things by art, magic, &c." He afterwards adds, " though this was the common report, I never lost a farthing by them, though I was with them several times." Pasquier afterwards says of his own knowledge—that the Gypsies had then been wandering up and down, under the eye and with the knowledge of the magistrates, for more than a hundred years. At length, in 1561, an edict was issued, banishing them out of that country. They are said to be very numerous in Lorraine and Alsace, where they found shelter in the forests in spite of edicts and orders of council.

Twiss describes them as being in great numbers in Spain, particularly Murcia, Cordova, &c. " Their language," he says, " which is peculiar to themselves, is everywhere so similar, that they are undoubtedly all derived from the same source. They began to appear in Europe in the fifteenth century, and are probably a mixture of Egyptians and Ethiopians. It is supposed that there are upwards of forty thousand of them in Spain ; great numbers of them are innkeepers in villages ; they are everywhere fortune-tellers. **** " Most of them have a smattering of physic and surgery, and are skilful in tricks performed by sleight of hand." In refutation of the charge of their being thieves he says, " I have lodged many times in their houses, and never missed the most trifling thing, though I have left my knives, forks, spoons, and linen at their mercy."

Swinburne says, that they swarm in the province of Grenada. All the Gypsies that he conversed with, assured him that they were sound Catholics ; but they were not generally esteemed such. In Calabria he found great numbers : he says of them, that they only contract marriages among themselves ; that they support life by profits of handicrafts ; but more by swapping asses and horses. That they generally work in iron and make trivets, knitting needles, bodkins, and such trifles :—that their religion is locked up in their own bosoms :— that they seem to have no great veneration for the Virgin Mary, but are supposed to believe in Christ : —that if the priests start any objection respecting marrying, christening, &c. they manage the matter in their own way, without giving them any farther trouble. In 1560 they were banished ; and again in 1569 and 1583, but with little effect.

Grillmann describes them as being found in all parts of Italy ; being most numerous in the dominions of the Church, there being the most superstition, and the worst police. A general law throughout Italy, forbad them remaining more than two nights in a place. This was found to be no great inconvenience to *them*, though it proved considerably so to the stationary inhabitants. He asserts, that the Gypsies are exceedingly numerous in Poland and Lithuania, as well as in Courland ; that they are found in Denmark and Sweden ; and that in Hungary there are upwards of fifty thousand of them. Cantemar says, that they are dispersed all over Moldavia, where every baron has several families of them. In Wallachia and the Sclavonian mountains they are very numerous, as well as in Bessarabia, Tartary, Bulgaria, Greece, and Romania; and that in Constantinople they greatly abound. They are spread throughout Russia in great abundance. In many parts of Asia they are very numerous. Grillmann supposes that on a moderate computation the number of Gypsies in Europe and Asia may be seven or eight hundred thousand. The probability is, that this is very greatly under the mark. In "An account of Wallachia and Moldavia," lately published by William Wilkinson, Esq., late British Consul to those two principalities, it is stated, that there are in them alone, at this day, one hundred and fifty thousand Gypsies.

When Gypsies originally arrived in England is very uncertain. They are first noticed in our laws, by several statutes against them in the reign of Henry VIII.; in which they are described as "an outlandish people, calling themselves *Egyptians;* who do not profess any craft or trade, but go about in great numbers, from place to place, using insidious and underhand means to impose on his Majesty's subjects, making them believe that they understand the art of foretelling men and women their good and evil fortune, by looking into their hands, whereby they defraud people of their money." It then proceeds to lay a penalty of forty pounds on any one *importing* any such Egyptian. During the same reign numbers of them were shipped at the public expense to France. They were calculated then to amount to ten thousand in England. Repeated statutes have since been passed against them, but with little effect. In Scotland they appear to have been much more numerous. In almost all countries in Europe severe enactments against them have, at different times, been passed ; such enactments have, however, in no instance been attended with the desired effect. This may easily be accouuted for : in the first place, they were not possessed, like the Jews, of property to repay their persecuters for the trouble and expense of prosecution. They had no natural home,. to which any country had a right to send them ; and in the next place their habits of life were such, as to enable them almost to set at defiance all such efforts to expel them. No part of the country was too desolate for them to exist, or even enjoy themselves in ; and in those days such desolate parts were to be met with abundantly in every country. Hence it has been, that all attempts to expel them have always proved abortive.

From the knowledge which they seem all to have possessed, of every region in which they have been first noticed, it is evident that they must have been, at that time, long resident there. They were not only acquainted with the languages of each nation, but they appear to have been well apprized of the several failings of the inhabitants. They had the sagacity to discern, and the ingenuity to take advantage of their several weaknesses. They had likewise taken up the practice of such trades as were adapted to their own habits, and likely at the

same time to afford them a livelihood in their
adopted country. These things evidently prove
that their residence in the different parts of Europe
must have been many ages prior to any account of
them which has reached us.

There never appears to have been, any surmise
of their origin being different to what they themselves assert it to have been, viz., Egyptian, but one,
and that seems only to have been taken up on the
ground of some similarity of language; that one
is, that they are of the lowest caste of Hindoos
from the East. This similarity of language does
not militate against their descent from the ancient
Egyptians, as it is very probable that both languages, viz, the Egyptian and Hindoo, may have
sprung from the same root. This supposition, as
being the only one at variance with that which I
have adopted, it may be well to examine; especially as it has been taken up by most late writers
on the subject. On this supposition, a miraculous
interference has never been pretended; it must
therefore rest on its natural grounds, and on them,
I think, it may be shewn to be *impossible*.

The Gypsies have, by the above-mentioned
writers, been supposed to have been *Soudras* driven
to forsake their native country by the cruelties of
Timour Beg, in the years 1408—9.* The affinity
of the two languages is the only ground on which
this opinion is supported. The only evidences of
this which have been adduced are a list of a few

* The Gypsies must have been in Europe long before
that time.

D

words which sound something alike in both languages.   No single according sentence has yet, I
believe, ever been produced.   Now it is evident
from the Gypsy language being still the same with
them in all countries, that *it* has not changed, nor
is it probable that the Hindostanee has been mate-
rially altered ; if so, the Soudras and the Gypsies
could understand each other ; but it has never
been asserted that they do.   It is by no means
improbable, however, as before noted, that on the
supposition of the Gypsies being from Egypt, the
two languages may have sprung from the same
root.

  Against the Gypsies being Soudras, or any caste
of Hindoos, the following reasons may be urged as
conclusive :—It is well known that the Soudras are,
and always were, among the most abject of the
human race. Oppressed and spiritless ; held in ab-
horrence, and treated with contempt, by all the other
castes of their countrymen ; their touch, and even
presence being considered as contaminating. Now
though it is possible that such a people as this
might be roused by oppression to resistance, and if
successful, to take signal vengeance on their oppressors ; it is not possible that they should be the
first to fear or to flee a revolutionary conqueror.
No change could render their condition more in-
tolerable ; *any* change might make it better.   In
all probability, they would be the first and the loud-
est in lauding a successful adventurer, and the last
to flee from him, especially to seek refuge they
knew not where, and from they knew not what.

Suppose, however, for argument's sake, that tens, if not hundreds of thousands, of these poor wretches *had* determined to fly from their native country, and men, women, and children, all born slaves, had been suffered to depart, whither were they to go? It is not probable that they could know of any country beyond their own; much less could they know the way to Europe; and yet they must all have immediately combined in one systematic plan of operations, to emigrate to that distant quarter of the world. But suppose this all done; they must, at any rate, have to travel through Persia, Arabia, and Egypt, more than two thousand miles. Suppose that six or eight hundred thousand half-naked defenceless wretches could have been suffered to cross these extensive and populous countries, how were they to be subsisted on their way? No country, unprepared for their reception, could, if inclined, provision them. But suppose that they had, by some means or other, reached the shores of the Mediterranean, what possible inducement could they have for crossing it? They could know nothing of countries lying beyond it. If, however, they were resolved on the experiment, where were the ships? Hundreds, solely appointed for the purpose, would have been necessary. If they had, by any imaginable means, got to Europe, they must all have then agreed to divide, each party having their own station appointed them, and each party must travel to their respective countries, even to the utmost peninsular point of Europe; and all this without any of them knowing the language of any one of the very numerous countries, through which they had to emigrate.

The idea of the possibility of such a case does really appear too absurd to be sincerely entertained. The objections, however, against it, are far from being yet all stated. The manners and customs of the two people were, from the first, as dissimilar as light and darkness. The Soudras are the most abject of the human race, cringing before all other men, as creatures of an inferior nature ; submitting without resistance, or even complaining, to the vilest offices and the most tyrannical treatment. The Gypsies, on the contrary, from the first accounts of them which have reached us, even during the time of Timour Beg, have been distinguished by a most unconquerable spirit of independence, and an untameable love of liberty. This spirit has never been conquered, this love has never forsaken them ! The Soudras were as ignorant as they were abject. The Gypsies have always been distinguished for ingenuity, a knowledge of the world and of human nature, which has enabled them to take advantages of circumstances, and to profit by the weaknesses and prejudices of others.

The ideas of the Soudras on religious subjects would be the most gross that could be conceived. Those of the Gypsies are the most simple ; they have no idols—no religious ceremonies, nor any superstitious notions or observances. This circumstance (miraculous intervention out of the question) must preclude the possibility of the Gypsies being originally Hindoos. The multiplicity of the gods of the latter people is perhaps beyond all comparison greater than those of any other : yet tens of thousands of the most ignorant of these superstitious idolaters leave their own country together, they separate into distinct clans, all carrying their household gods with them, and disperse into diverse countries, never seeing each other more, yet every clan, as by common consent, casting away from them their gods, their superstitious observances, their idolatrous worship, and all of them becoming, at one and the same time, free, not only from their own forms of religious worship, but from all forms whatever. This does seem to be utterly impossible ! This freedom from idolatrous worship is indeed of itself a circumstance so totally contrary to all that experience has shown us of human nature under similar circumstances, that nothing less than miraculous interposition is sufficient to account for it. On the supposition then, and that alone, of the Gypsies being the descendants of the dispersed Egyptians can these difficulties be got over.

We know that the Jews coming from the neighbouring country to Egypt, have continued to this day a distinct, though dispersed people. Supposing, then, a Divine interposition, there are no difficulties attaching to the state of one people more than to that of the others.

Of the works of that long lost people, the ancient Egyptians, the more they become known the more astonishing and interesting do they appear to be. Most awful and impressive is the lesson, which, under any view of them, they afford to this generation; but how exceedingly would the awfulness and impressiveness of that lesson be increased, should it appear that the houseless, friendless, despised and persecuted Gypsies, who have for ages lived and been held among us in contempt, are the descendants of the very people by whom those mighty works, at which we are so astonished, were formed! It would almost seem as if all these discoveries had been permitted to be made, and this attention to be excited at this time, to increase the interest which this people now claim. They have hitherto excited little curiosity, yet they have always asserted that the land which contains these stupendous works, was the land of their forefathers. In making this assertion they could not be actuated by any self-interested or improper motive. They knew nothing but the name of the country which they claimed as their own. If that claim conferred any thing upon them, it was only additional contempt.

MODERN EGYPT.

" The land of Egypt is a land of wonders !
And sure that eye were dead to all attractions,
That would not see, or seeing, saw unmoved,
This Memphian miracle of ancient skill—
The Nile, the lotus'd Nile, of reverend story—
The Sphynx—the hieroglyphic obelisks—
The ruin'd catacombs—old Pharaoh's palace,
All, all the wrecks and symbols thrown about
This broken cradle of the infant arts."

HOLLAND.

FORTY years ago, Egypt would have been among
the very last countries that would have been judged
likely to become the stage of actions peculiarly interesting to the inhabitants of Europe, and particularly to those of this kingdom, a kingdom so
detached and so remotely situated from it. Yet
within that short period it has been brought most
highly to interest the different nations of Europe,
but particularly the English nation. From the
highest to the lowest, from the old to the young ;
from the most learned to the most illiterate ; from

the soldier to the priest ; from the grave antiquary
to the dashing young nobleman ; from the philosopher to the school-boy ; all have of late been,
more or less, interested in the transactions and the
discoveries occurring in that remote country. Who
could have imagined, half a century ago, that
Egypt would be the country to which the armies
and navies of England and France would be transported, at an enormous expense, to fight their
battles ; to dye the waters of Africa with their
blood, and to whiten the fields of that distant
quarter of the world, with their bones ? Who
would have imagined that such a man as Buona-
parte would have appeared, to compel the attention
of all the civilized world to that desolate country ;
or, that such a man as Belzoni would sojourn there
to discover, to describe, and, in fact, to convey to
this country, works of art, more extraordinary and
stupendous than almost any with which the world
was before acquainted ?—works which have attracted
and rivetted the attention of persons of all degrees,
ages, and acquirements, to Egypt and its inhabitants, both in their present and former state, in a
degree beyond whatever could have been imagined
possible. Who would have conceived that, of all
these interesting and astonishing works, *this* country, a country divided from *that* by almost a quarter
of the globe, should become the depository, at least
of such of them as were believed capable and
worthy of being removed ; nay even of many
which were then thought to be beyond the strength
or art of man to convey so far ? All these things

seem to point out this country as the proper place from whence inquiries relating to Egypt should proceed ; and this as the proper time when such information as is required should be disseminated.

The Marquis Spineto, in his lectures on Egyptian Antiquities, says :—" In considering these astonishing productions we must really wonder how a nation, which was so great as to erect these stupendous edifices, could so far fall into oblivion, that even their language and method of writing are unknown to us. But our wonder will, if possible, increase to a higher degree when we take into consideration the materials which have been so modelled. They had only four sort of stones in general use for sculptures ; the sandy, the calcareous, the breccia, and the granite. All, excepting the first, are very hard ; and what is more singular, we do not know with what tools they were cut. We know by experience that the tools of the present day will not cut granite without great difficulty : and Belzoni, who had made so many experiments on this stone, doubts whether we could give it the smoothness and surface which we see in Egypt. On the calcareous stones the figures have angles so sharp, that the best tempered chisels of our times could not produce the like. It is so hard that it breaks more like glass than stone, and yet with these materials they have produced the most exquisite specimens of architecture and sculpture ; for in both these arts their productions have a boldness of execution that has never been equalled by any other nation. The gigantic statues of Greece and Rome are but dwarfs and pigmies when compared to those of Karnac, Luxor, Esne, Dandera, and indeed of the whole of Egypt and Nubia.

" They had made besides considerable progress in several manufactures, even to a degree which is really astonishing. Their linen manufacture had a perfection equal to our own. In many of their figures we observe their garments quite transparent; and among the folding of the mummies, Belzoni observed cloth quite as fine as our common muslin, being very strong and of an equal texture. They had also the art of tanning leather, and staining it with various colours, as we do morocco, and actually knew the mode of embossing it. Many specimens of the sort have been found with figures impressed on the leather quite raised. The same may be said of their art in making glass, some of which was of a beautiful black colour, and so perfect, as to resemble the natural obsidian. Of such glass was made the celebrated statue of Menelaus. This information we gather from Pliny, who makes use of this observation to prove that the art of manufacturing glass was very ancient. Besides enamelling, the art of gilding was in great perfection among them, and they knew how to beat gold nearly as thin as ours, for Belzoni found many ornaments of the kind, and a leaf of gold which appeared to him to be very fine, and of a brighter colour than we often see. They knew also how to cast copper, and to form it into sheets, and they had a metallic composition not unlike our lead, but of greater tenacity. Carved works were very common, and in great perfection, particularly in the proportion of their figures : and the art of varnishing, and baking the varnish on clay, was in such perfection, that the most enlightened travellers have doubted whether they could be equalled at present. I have already noticed their skill and perfection in painting, and in the blending of the colours. Indeed the more I consider what they have done, and what they were capable of doing, the more I am lost in amazement; for as most of the stupendous works are of the highest antiquity, they must have been the production, of their artists, in the hierarchic government, and so near to the deluge, that, even adopting our older system of the Septuagint chronology, a man can hardly conceive how a nation could in so short a time render habitable the whole valley of the Nile, and acquire such knowledge, and make so great a proficiency in most sciences, and in most manufactures, and in all the arts."

A few extracts from Belzoni's narrative of discoveries and operations in Egypt, may serve to shew more clearly the ancient and present state of that extraordinary part of the world, and to increase in a proportionate degree the interest and the importance of the subject of this work.

Respecting " *the City of the Hundred Gates*" Belzoni thus writes—" On the 22d, we saw for the first time the ruins of the great Thebes, and landed at Luxor. Here I beg the reader to observe that but very imperfect ideas can be formed of the extensive ruins of Thebes, even from the accounts of

the most skilful and accurate travellers.   It is impossible to imagine the scene displayed without
seeing it.   The most sublime ideas that can be
formed, from the most magnificent specimens of
our present architecture, would give a very incorrect picture of these ruins ; for such is the difference, not only in magnitude, but in form, proportion, and construction, that even the pencil can
convey but a faint idea of the whole.   It appeared
to me like entering a city of giants, who, after a
long conflict were all destroyed, leaving the ruins
of their various temples as the only proofs of their
former existence.

" The temple of Luxor presents to the traveller
at once one of the most splendid groups of
Egyptian grandeur.   The extensive propyleon,
with the two obelisks and colossal statues in the
front ; the thick groups of enormous columns ; the
variety of apartments, and the sanctuary it contains ; the beautiful ornaments which adorn every
part of the walls and columns described by Mr.
Hamilton ; cause in the astonished traveller, an
oblivion of all that he has seen before.   If his
attention be attracted to the north side of Thebes,
by the towering remains that project a great height
above the palm-trees, he will gradually enter that
forestlike assemblage of ruins of temples, wherein
are obelisks, colossi, Sphynxes, portals, and an
endless number of other astonishing objects, that
will convince him at once of the impossibility of a
description.

" On the west side of the Nile, still the traveller

finds himself among wonders. The temples of
Goumore, Memnonium, and Medinet Aboo, attest
the extent of the Great City on that side. The
unrivalled colossal figures in the plain of Thebes,
the number of tombs excavated in the rocks,
those in the great valley of the kings, with their
paintings, sculptures, mummies, sarcophagi, figures,
&c., are all objects worthy of the admiration of the
traveller, *who will not fail to wonder how a nation,
which was once so great as to erect these stupendous
edifices, could so far fall into oblivion, that even
their language and writings are totally unknown
to us.*"

The bust only, of the statue of Memnon, now
deposited in the British Museum, weighs not less
than ten or twelve tons. The following is the description of the exterior of the temple of Ipsam-
bul :—" It is one hundred and seventeen feet wide,
and eighty-six feet high ; the height from the top
of the cornice to the top of the door being sixty-
six feet six inches, and the height of the door
twenty feet. There are four enormous sitting
colossi, the largest in Egypt or Nubia, except the
great Sphynx at the pyramids, to which they approach in the proportion of nearly two-thirds.
From the shoulder to the elbow they measure fifteen feet six inches ; the ears three feet six inches ;
the face seven feet ; the beard five feet six inches ;
across the shoulders twenty feet four inches : their
height is about fifty-one feet, not including the caps,
which are about fourteen feet. There are only two
of these colossi in sight ; one is still buried under

the sand, and the other, which is near the door, is
half fallen down and buried also.   On the top of
the door, is a colossal figure of Osiris, twenty feet
high, with two colossal hieroglyphic figures, one on
each side looking towards it.   On the top of the
temple is a cornice with hieroglyphics, a torus, and
frieze under it.   The cornice is six feet wide, the
frieze four feet.   Above the cornice, is a row of
sitting monkeys, eight feet high and six across the
shoulders.   They are twenty-one in number.   This
temple was nearly two-thirds buried under the sand,
of which we removed thirty-one feet before we
came to the upper part of the door.   It must have
had a very fine landing place, which is now totally
buried under the sand."

This temple is only one of many other such, excavated out of the solid rock, in different parts of
Egypt.   The interior is in corresponding style of
vast magnificence.   "We entered" says the in-
defatigable Belzoni, "into a large pronaos fifty-
seven feet long, and fifty-two wide, supported by
two rows of square pillars, in a line from the front
door to the door of the sekos.   Each pillar has a
figure not unlike those at Medinet Aboo, finely
executed and very little injured by time.   The
tops of their turbans reach the ceiling which is
about thirty feet high : the pillars are five feet and
a half square.   Both these and the walls are
covered with beautiful hieroglyphics, the style of
which is somewhat superior, or at least bolder, than
that of any others [known] in Egypt, not only in
workmanship, but also in the subjects.   They

exhibit battles, storming of castles, triumphs over
the Ethiopians, sacrifices, &c., &c." The numerous other rooms, all of which are minutely
described, are in a corresponding style of sublime
grandeur.

The tombs which Mr. Belzoni examined were
almost innumerable. The expense, the care, and
the constant attention paid by the Egyptians to
their dead, were, he observes, "almost incredible."
Many of the bodies appeared to have been carefully wrapped in linen of different degrees of fine-
ness, at different and distant periods. "In some
of the chambers of the tombs were the mummies
of cows, sheep, monkeys, crocodiles, bats, and other
animals, intermixed with human bodies; and one
tomb was filled with nothing but cats, carefully
folded in red and white linen, the head covered by
a mask representing the cat, and made of the same
linen."

The danger, the difficulties, and the unpleasant-
ness of visiting these mansions of the deed of former
ages, is thus interestingly described by the daunt-
less traveller :—"Of some of these tombs, many
persons could not withstand the suffocating air
which often causes fainting. A vast quantity of
dust rises so fine that it penetrates the throat and
nostrils, and chokes the nose and mouth to such a
degree, that it requires great power of lungs to resist it and the strong effluvia of the mummies. This
is not all, the passages where the bodies are, are
roughly cut in the rocks, and the falling of the sand
from the upper part of the ceiling of the passage

causes it to be nearly filled up. In some places there is not more than the vacancy of a foot left, which you must contrive to pass through in a creeping posture like a snail, on pointed and keen stones that cut like glass. After getting through three passages, some of them two or three hundred yards long, you generally find a more commodious place, perhaps high enough to sit. But what a place of rest! surrounded by bodies, by heaps of mummies in all directions, which, previous to my being accustomed to the sight, impressed me with horror. The blackness of the walls, the faint light given by the candles or torches, for want of air, the different objects that surrounded me, seeming to converse with each other, and the Arabs with the candles or torches in their hands, naked and covered with dust, themselves resembling living mummies, absolutely formed a scene that cannot be described. In such a situation I found myself several times, and often returned exhausted and fainting, till at last I became inured to it, and indifferent to what I suffered, except from the dust, which never failed to choak my throat and nose; though fortunately I am destitute of the sense of smelling, I could *taste* that the mummies were *rather unpleasant to swallow*.

" After the exertion of entering into such a place through a passage of fifty, a hundred, three hundred, or perhaps six hundred yards, nearly overcome, I sought a resting place, found one, and contrived to sit; but when my weight bore on the body of an Egyptian, it crushed in like a band-box.

I naturally had recourse to my hands to sustain my
weight, but they found no better support ; so that
I sunk altogether among the broken mummies, with
a crash of bones, rags, and wooden cases, which
raised such a dust as kept me motionless for a quarter of an hour, waiting till it subsided again. I
could not remove from the place, however, without
increasing it, and every step that I took I crushed
a mummy in some part or other. Once I was conducted from such a place to another resembling it,
through a passage about twenty feet in length, and
no wider than that a body could be forced through.
It was choked with mummies, and I could not pass
without putting my face in contact with that of
some decayed Egyptian ; but as the passage inclined downwards my own weight helped me on ;
however I could not avoid being covered with bones,
heads, arms, and legs rolling from above. Thus I
proceeded from one cave to another, all full of
mummies piled up in various ways, some standing,
some lying, and some on their heads. The purpose
of my researches was to rob the Egyptians of their
papyri, of which I found a few hidden in their
breasts, under their arms, in the space above their
knees, or on their legs, and covered by the numerous folds of cloth that envelope the mummy. The
people of Gournou who made a trade of antiquities
of this sort, are very jealous of strangers, and keep
them as secret as possible, deceiving travellers by
pretending that they have arrived at the end of the
pits, when they are scarcely at their entrance. I

could never prevail on them to conduct me into these places before this, my second voyage, when I succeeded in obtaining admission into any caves where mummies were to be seen."

Other tombs were discovered, particularly in Bebal el Molook, even more capacious than these. Here it was that the unwearied searcher discovered a tomb, which he says, richly repaid him for the trouble and hazard that attended all his researches. The day on which he made the discovery he considers as the most fortunate of his life : and the tomb and its contents as the most superb and splendid remains of Egyptian antiquities. This tomb the traveller conceives to be that of Pharoah Necho, and the superb sarcophagus which was there found, and which is or was in the British Museum, he conceives to be the one which contained the body of a demi-god, the tempter of Israel to sin, of whom the Lord declared, " Behold I am against thee, Pharoah, King of Egypt, the great dragon that lieth in the midst of his rivers, which hath said, my river is mine own, and I have made it myself. But I will put hooks in thy jaws.

" I will leave thee thrown into the wilderness, thee and all the fish of thy rivers.

" Behold, therefore, I am against thy rivers, and I will make the land of Egypt utterly waste and desolate, from the tower of Syene, even unto the borders of Ethiopia.

" And I will make the land of Egypt desolate, even among the countries that are desolate, and her cities among the cities that are laid waste; and *I will scatter the Egyptians among the nations, and I will disperse them through the countries.*

Supposing, as there appear to be strong grounds to do, that the Gypsies are the descendants of the ancient Egyptians, what an awful and impressive fulfilment do they afford of these striking denunciations of the Divine wrath against a people and nation, *then* more powerful and splendid, than any nation upon the earth! The discovery of all these magnificent remains of the former grandeur of that people, and the discovery of the remnant of that people at this day "scattered among the nations, and fallen upon the open fields of the uncircumcised;" serve strikingly to illustrate and to fulfil these extraordinary predictions. The Gypsies are *now* outcasts even among the most despised people and nations.

The most striking productions of the arts, the most splendid ornaments of their palaces, their temples and their tombs, are brought and exhibited as objects of curiosity to a country of which they (the ancient Egyptians) had never heard the name: a country, whose inhabitants were then little better than naked painted savages, wandering wild in the depths of their forests. Among this people and nation, do the descendants of the proud Egyptians wander as outcast vagrants; while the gods and the idols of their forefathers, are there exhibited as mementos of God's power, and as objects to excite astonishment, commiseration, or scorn: the useless ornaments of palaces, or the play-things of children.

The bodies of their ancestors, their priests, their nobles, their kings and their queens, which they vainly imagined they had rendered immortal, immoveable, and undiscoverable, are now exhibited in that despised country, to the gaze and contempt of the lowest of the rabble; or are converted, it is affirmed, into nauseous sickening medicines, for the cure of loathsome diseases.

If such things and occurrences as these were predicted more than two thousand years ago to happen, and have now (as then predicted) come to pass, surely it must be *the Lord's doing!* That such events were then predicted, we do know from unquestionable authority! That such occurrences are now taking place, we have the testimony of our senses to prove. Let us, then, neither shut our eyes nor our ears, nor wilfully withhold the free exercise of our understandings, and we cannot, I think, remain either uninterested or unconvinced!

The whole description of this wonderful and splendid tomb of Pharaoh Necho, and the sarcophagus which was supposed to have contained the body of that monarch (long since stolen and probably destroyed,) are highly interesting. As, however, the sarcophagus itself is now in this country, and an exact model of the different apartments of the wonderful tomb has been there exhibited, it is unnecessary to insert the description of them here.

All these things serve to shew, that the descriptions of the magnificence and power of the Egyptians have not been exaggerated either by sacred or profane historians. The accounts furnished by

Belzoni and other travellers shew, that the degree
of desolation and misery predicted by the prophets
to fall upon Egypt, was not beyond what is now
seen and experienced in that country ; and the present condition of the Gypsies affords, in almost every
country of Europe, and even America, an instance
of a people claiming to be Egyptians, in circumstances fully corresponding with those predicted to
happen to that race of human beings. The countenances, the complexion, and the assertions of the
Gypsies, all corroborate the supposition of their
being that scattered people, who are to be brought,
eventually, out of every country whither they were
driven, and in the open fields of which they were
dispersed ; that people, whom the Lord will cause
to return unto the land of Pathros, and into the
land of their habitation, there to know Him. " In
that day there shall be an altar to the Lord in the
midst of Egypt, and a pillar at the border thereof
to the Lord ; and it shall be for a sign, and for a
witness unto the Lord of Hosts, in the land of
Egypt ; for they shall cry unto the Lord because
of the oppressors, and He shall send them a Saviour
and a Great One, and He shall deliver them. And
the Lord shall be known to Egypt, and the Egyptians shall know the Lord in that day, and shall do
sacrifice and oblation : yea, they shall vow a vow
unto the Lord, and shall perform it. And the Lord
shall smite Egypt, he shall smite it and heal it ;
and they shall return even to the Lord, and He
shall be entreated of them, and shall heal them."
Isaiah, chapter xix.

ENGLISH GYPSIES.

"Yet are they here?—the same unbroken knot
Of human beings, in the self-same spot?
    Men, women, children, yea the very frame
    Of the whole spectacle the same!
Only their fire seems bolder, yielding light;
Now deep and red, the colouring of night;
    That on their Gipsy-faces falls,
    Their bed of straw and blanket-walls."
WORDSWORTH.

IF we examine the character and conduct of the Gypsies, as they exist this day in England, they will be found to be much less objectionable than is generally imagined; the same observation, I believe, will apply, in a great measure, to those in all other countries. They appear to me to be a people "more sinned against than sinning." Their better peculiarities have always been overlooked; while those more objectionable ones, through the results of the peculiar circumstances in which they are placed, have even been exaggerated, misrepresented, and multiplied, by prejudice and inhumanity. We call them rogues and vagabonds; we treat them

as if they were such ; thereby doing our best to
make and keep them so. The crimes of which they
have geneially been accused, and for which they
have been punished, have, for the most part, been
such as could not be considered as crimes by them.
They have been vilified, hunted from place to place.
driven to banishment, prison, and death, for leading
a life to which they were born—from which they
had no inclination, no divine command to depart,
but to which, on the contrary, they were, perhaps,
decreed by the fiat of the Almighty ; yet, for this
has every man's tongue and every man's hand been
against them.   What it might have been possible
to have made of them, had they been treated with
humanity and kindness, it is yet impossible to say,
because the experiment has, unfortunately, never
been tried in any country ; although they have resided in all parts of Europe, at least four or five
hundred years.   I will not admit the attempt of
the Empress Theresa, in 1773, to be of that description ; though the state was at the expense of carrying off waggon-loads of children, torn from the arms
of their distracted parents, to attempt to civilize and
Christianize them.   No wonder that the attempt
should fail !

Those things considered, it is not to be wondered
at, that the Gypsies have not become Christians.
What they have seen and experienced, of the effects
of Christianity, unfortunately for the credit of that
religion, have not been such as to cause them to
think well either of it, or of its professors : that
they have not been driven to hate and to shun

them, seems the most surprising. This, however, has not been the case; to some of the rites of Christianity, the Gypsies in this country conform, and, with its professors they would, I believe, gladly live in peace.

Generally speaking, there seems a peculiar steadiness and sedateness in the manners and the conduct of the Gypsies, which keeps them alike from cringing and presuming. They are a silent and reflecting people—levity of conduct is rarely seen, even among the younger Gypsies. Though often practitioners on musical instruments, they are rarely, if ever, heard singing or whistling in that way which bespeaks lightness of heart. They are not in the general habit of dancing, and are rarely heard to laugh. It is a very extraordinary peculiarity, in a people circumstanced us they are, that *they have no poetry whatever* in their own language, nor do they seem to regard it in any other. They know nothing of painting, or any of the arts of embellishment. They have no tales of any kind, which they repeat to their children—no legends, no exploits of their forefathers, no recitations to arouse the passions, or stimulate to exertion, to amuse or to enliven. They are of course no readers, yet they do not pass their time idly smoking. They are not drunkards or even habitual drinkers; occasionally some of them are known to drink to excess, but not frequently; their character in that respect is that of sobriety. They are peculiarly abstemious in eating, and, indeed, in all their habits. Their habitations, their clothing, their food, are

E

alike simple, coarse, and scanty in the extreme :
for the latter the very refuse and offal of what is
consumed by others, even the dead carcases of animals which they find by the way side, frequently
suffice to satisfy them.   Let them but enjoy unmolested their dear loved liberty and independence,
among the wilds of nature, and they seem to set
the effects of hunger, of cold, and nakedness, at
defiance.

It is, perhaps, this abstemiousness and disregard
of the comforts and even necessaries of life, which,
more than their evil practices, have served to cause
them to be considered as universal depredators.
Christians accustomed to many comforts and enjoyments for which the poor Gypsies never look, cannot imagine that they can subsist so contentedly
without them ; they therefore conclude that the
Gypsies have them and obtain them unfairly.   I
doubt that too many of their accusers feel conscious
that they themselves, under similar circumstances
would be tempted to dishonest acts ; hence it is concluded by them, that the Gypsies are what they
themselves feel they should be in their situation.
Let it be understood, that there are rogues and
vagabonds of the worst description, *personating
Gypsies, and often passing for them,* and it is not
improbable but the most of those who have been
convicted of the greater crimes, have been of that
description of vagrants.   I have had, and heard
of, the testimony of many respectable gentlemen,
farmers, and others, near whose premises the Gypsies have long been in the habit of encamping,

borne to their honesty, having never had reason to suppose that they robbed them of any thing. While those who have treated them with kindness, by letting them encamp unmolested on their waste grounds, and giving them straw or any small matters, have found them rather protectors than destroyers of their property.*

The Gypsies, I believe, rarely under any circumstances apply for parochial relief; their independence of spirit and abstemious habits incline and enable them to do without it. This is an example worthy of being imitated by many of their traducers. Another favourable peculiarity of theirs is, that they are rarely if ever seen as common beggars. On the late investigation throughout London and Westminister one only instance occurred, and

---

* The Author has lately received the following note from a friend :—

SIR,—I was in company a few days ago, with a gentleman residing at Duckmanton, near Chesterfield, who was relating a recent circumstance in that neighbourhood, which recalled your interesting work on the Gypsies to my recollection. Circumscribed as it is, it may not be wholly unworthy your regard; during the late floods, a farmer in the vicinity was aroused in the night by a Gypsy from an encampment not far distant, informing him that the rising waters were carrying off the sheep from his pastures. The farmer hastened with all the help he could to the place, where the Gypsy people were then using every exertion in his behalf; by *their means*, only seventeen (out of the seventy-five carried away) were lost. You will excuse this mite—though small, it is not wholly chaff. I am, Sir, very respectfully, yours,

————.",

even that a doubtful one.   The females, I believe,
are rarely, if ever, found among those dreadful pests
to society in large towns, common prostitutes.
Their parental and filial affection is said to be exemplary : their aged parents they tend to the last
with a care and attention not often witnessed in
polished society ; and they are accused of being
indulgent to their children even to an injurious excess ; refusing to correct them for faults which
clearly demand it.   The Gypsies are allowed to be
susceptible of the most lively and lasting gratitude.
Wherever particular kindness has been shewn to
them by any individual, their affectionate sense
of the favour seems to have known no bounds.
Many instances of this are on record.   A very
strong one is related in the case of the late Mr.
Nesbit, of Roxburghshire, who was accustomed to
be indulgent to them, and to call them his *body-
guard.*   In all their engagements, they are said to
be scrupulously punctual, especially when confidence seems to have been placed in their promises ;
but whenever their word has been doubted, or a
want of confidence evinced, they have shewn themselves strongly offended.   It is urged against them,
that they marry within the line of consanguinity, and
that they sleep the whole family promiscuously together under the cover of their little tent.   These
have been the piactices, in all cases, in the early
stages of society ; they are inseparable from it.   In
something approaching to that state, the Gypsies
still remain.   The indecorum, then, to them is not
perceptible, and being no law, there is no sin.   It

is probable that they sleep together in their clothes, as innocently as more polished parties often *sit* together. As to their being fortune-tellers, it is much less disgraceful to them, than to those whose ignorance (or wickedness) encourages them to such practices.

The Gypsies are by far more intelligent and ci- vilized than the depraved part of the lower ranks in large towns. Let any one, who has opportunity, look at such, and compare them with the Gypsies ; the comparison will little redound to the credit of the former. See the mechanics at their work, surly and dissatisfied with themselves their condition, their employers, their relievers, their rulers, and with every thing around them ; dirty, offensive, unhealthy, and miserable ; un- willingly, and with murmuring, performing that labour which God hath appointed as the needful task of all men on earth. Hear them, in almost every sentence that they utter, cursing and blas- pheming, calling upon God to bear witness to the grossest falsehoods, while, in language the most profane and indecent, they ridicule every thing that is sacred and chaste. Follow them to the ale- house, and hear all this repeated amidst the roar of drunkenness ; follow them from thence, if you have sufficient courage and resolution, home to their wives and children,—but if you have, I must leave you to go without me ; I have seen them there too often ; my heart sickens at the recollection, and I cannot, without a stronger motive than curiosity again pass their threshold.

To turn from the view of such a scene as this which has been described, to the contemplation of the family in the simple tent of the wandering Gypsy, is like exchanging the close and offensive lazar-house, for the fresh and smiling fields, and the glorious firmament of heaven. Who would not, after this, look on the comparatively innocent sons and daughters of rude wild nature, with feelings of satisfaction and almost with envy? The tempest may rage above the Gypsies' humble dwelling; the sleet may drive over or through the hedge that screens them; or the snow may be drifted up against them. The rain may fall in torrents upon their tents, or the loud thunder may crash over their heads—yet *within* there may be comfort and peace. That little frail dome, may cover an aged matron, a father and a mother, with six or eight children of different ages and sexes, and their beds may be little more than the cold bare ground, and yet they may be something like a family of love. I cannot, for the life of me, bring myself to despise them; they seem to me like the houseless birds whom God feedeth, and for whom He cares. They appear more than any other human beings to depend on Him alone for daily bread. They know not, it is true, much of Him: the wisest of us know but little more. They, however, may view Him in his wonders, and love to live amidst his works, and if they less adore, they, probably, less offend.

> " What a happy life we lead,
>   Free to wander where we please,

Like the wild colts in the mead,
Like the squirrels in the trees.

" God provides us all we want,
We on none but *Him* depend ;
Small imports what *man* can grant,
God Himself the Gypsy's friend."

Since my attention has been called to the subject of the Gypsies, I have of course been desirous
of embracing every opportunity of meeting with
them. I was lately informed of there being some
within a mile or two of my residence : I took the
first opportunity of visiting them. I found that
there was only one tent, and that the inmates consisted but of a man about twenty-six years of age
—his wife, a little younger, to whom he had been
married about six months, and his sister, not more
than twenty. Their names were Boswell, having
a few years before left their paternal tribe, and
started as the germ of a new one. The tent was
pitched in a retired green lane, a little way from a
considerable village. When it was all covered in,
it had the appearance of a long tilt for a huckster's
cart. One-third of it, in the middle, being un-
covered, the open space served as a kitchen, the
fire being made in it, and the two ends as separate
sleeping rooms. The whole apparatus was in good
repair.

When we first called (my daughter being with
me,) the young woman only was at home. She
had been washing, and the clothes were hung out
to dry on the hedges on each side of the road

We were greatly surprised to see them all equal in quality and colour to what one would expect to be worn by decent trades-people.   The appearance of the young woman, though thus busily employed, was neat and clean ; and, though her dress was not modern, it was strikingly graceful ; particularly the disposing of the coloured handkerchief as a kind of bandeau or turban round the head.   Her person was rather tall and highly elegant ; her eyes remarkably good, dark and piercing ; her features taken singly, not bad, while the expression of her countenance was strongly intelligent and peculiarly good humoured.   When she was addressed, she replied in language much above the vulgar, and in a tone which was soft and pleasing,   Her manners were unembarrassed, easy and cheerful, though perfectly modest and unassuming.   There was an appearance of respectability, comfort, order, and cleanliness throughout the whole of the little dwelling.   I presented her with a small work which I had some time before published, containing the " *Blind Man and his Son*," " *A Word for the Gypsies*," &c., and promised to call again when I thought her brother and sister would be at home.

In a day or two afterwards I called with a party of young ladies.   We found the Gypsies all at home.   The man was a fine figure, with an open, sensible, pleasing countenance.   His wife interesting both in person and face : her features, particularly the eyes and complexion, were not so decidedly those of Gypsies, as were those of the other two. She was not quite well, being, probably, as ladies wish to be at such times (six months after marriage,) who love their lords. The young ladies who accompanied me, were all exceedingly struck with the graceful figure, easy manners, pleasing countenance, refined language, and sweet tones of the young woman. They all declared that they had never seen any female before so interesting. The Gypsy party had just been taking tea, the apparatus for which was quite of the better kind, japanned tray, &c.; they invited us to be seated, and said that they should have been glad had we been in time to have taken tea with them. Two feather beds (with bed clothes good, and exceedingly clean,) laid on dry straw, occupied the two ends of the tent. As many of the young ladies as could find room reclined upon them with the Gypsy's wife. The young woman gracefully seated herself in the eastern fashion, and the man stood beside her. The group was altogether highly picturesque; a number of children, and one or two women from the neighbouring village, whom we found there, remained standing on the outside. The young woman, who seemed pleased with the children, said they were seldom without some of them, where they were known. I enquired if they found themselves frequently insulted or molested. She said, " Never ! for we endeavour to behave properly, and you know, Sir, that civility generally produces civility." I asked the man if he had read any book; he said no, he wished he could read, but he had never been taught. I promised

when they came again (they were going the next
day) to endeavour to have him put into a way of
learning—with this he appeared much pleased.

To the various questions which I put to him, he
told us that he had never heard any of their people
question their being originally from Egypt; he said
that he had heard that they were supposed by some
people to be from Hindoos, whose country he
seemed to imagine, was a part of Egypt. He believed that their language was everywhere the same
among them; he had never met with any that spoke
it any way different; but he did not know that
he had ever met with any Gypsies from foreign
parts; he never saw or heard of any book in their
language, though he had an uncle that he said was
learned, and could write. On my expressing a desire to see this uncle, he promised to try to arrange
with him some time so that I might have the opportunity. He never heard of any poetry whatever in their language, nor were they in the habit
of singing. They spoke English or Gypsy in-
discriminately among each other; he hardly knew,
he said, how the children learned to speak the
Gypsy language, they never took pains to teach
them; but added, smiling, " I think, Sir, *it seems
natural to them."* He obtained a livelihood by
selling tin goods, cutlery, and different kinds of
hardware.

I asked him, if it was true, as is generally said,
that the Gypsies prefer the flesh of animals that
have died a natural death, to that of those which
have been slaughtered. He knew of no such pre-

ference, but he said, with much feeling, " Sir, some of our people are very ill off, and are frequently glad of *anything* to eat." I asked him if he preferred their itinerant way of living in the open air, to that of residing in a house. A peculiar earnestness of expression shot into his countenance, and he replied with strong emphasis, and apparently with sincerity and devotion, " *Thank God!* that I am not compelled to live in the filth and foul air of towns." On this subject he seemed to like to dwell. He said we have every thing here, sweet and clean, and free from vermin of all kinds. We can go where we like ; we have no taxes to pay—we have very few cares ; we generally enjoy good health, and though in winter the weather is sometimes severe, it must be very much so to drive us into a house for shelter ; that was, however, the case last winter, and, for a little while, we were in lodgings at Birmingham. (I suspect he was married there at the time.) I asked if they were at one of the lodging-houses. He replied that nothing could drive them into such dreadful places ; that they had taken a small room for a few weeks, which they had entirely to themselves : but that he always felt the strongest repugnance to living in a house.

I had not an opportunity of making all the enquiries that I wished on the subject of religion. He said that whenever they were encamped near a village, in which there was a church, they generally went to it. That they preferred being married by a clergyman, but if that could not be con-

veniently accomplished, that they then " took one
another's word for it :" that he never knew a couple,
so married, that ever parted.   He and his wife
were married at church.

This was most of the conversation which I had
an opportunity of having with this interesting family.   He appeared to be freely communicative,
and said he should be glad to afford me any information in his power.   There was a steady, unembarrassed, but respectful freedom in his manner,
that was evidently the result of a consciousness of
independence, such as we rarely, if ever, meet with
among the lower classes in society.   At the same
time, they were all on the alert to shew their desire
to serve and to please.

I have not produced this little group as a fair
specimen of the Gypsy tribe.   I believe that it is
too favourable ; but it is the only one that has
offered itself to my observation, after I had taken
up my pen in their cause.   I have endeavoured
to sketch it clearly and accurately.   Both the outline
and the colouring are, I believe, pretty true to nature.

Ever since this extraordinary people have engaged so much of my attention and consideration,
I have wished for some opportunity of becoming
better acquainted with their habits, their manners,
and their language.   Since then I have been in
some degree, favoured with that opportunity.   In
taking my accustomed ride into the country, I met
with a tribe, or rather family, of Gypsies, consisting, as I then supposed, of the father, mother, and

five children ; it, however, proved, that the older of the children, a girl apparently about thirteen, was an orphan, and sister to the man, though probably nearly twenty years younger than he. I saw them several times, and at length asked the man if he would have any objections to leaving his sister with my family, at any rate, till he called again, which I understood would be in about eight days. Both he and the girl appeared very much pleased to embrace the offer. On asking if his sister understood the Gypsy language, he said, " O, yes, all the children can speak it." On asking him how they learned it, he replied, " O ! Sir, its natural to them. We never teach them, but they always can talk it." This idea seems to prevail among them all, that they speak the Gypsy language by something like instinct.

The man said his name was James *Vanis*. His sister's Clara Vanis. I have since heard that it was *Hearn*, and not Vanis. She was a slight well-formed girl, with a decidedly, but not strongly marked Gypsy countenance. Not handsome but strikingly intelligent. She spent the eight days with us, and obtained much of the admiration, and almost affection of every inmate of the family. Without any thing approaching to forwardness, or boldness, she was free from any embarrasing timidity. Though every thing about her was of course novel and striking, a proper sense of which she expressed, yet she never appeared to act as if in an element to which she had never been accustomed ; nor, when dressed in better clothes, did they ap-

pear either to embarrass her, or to attract much
of her attention. With the servants, she was
soon a favourite. Obliging and attentive to all,
she requested that they would keep her always
employed, and and she went about all the house
business to which she was set, in a way that appeared as if she had been long accustomed to it.
She could sew very tolerably. She soon learned
to milk, with which she was much pleased. Her
brother being a tinker, brazier, tinner, umbrella-
mender, &c. &c. &c., she had acquired a knowledge
and expertness which few servants possess. She
was cheerful and merry with the servants, expressing her happiness in her new situation, and frequently contrasting it with her old one. On their
asking her if she should be glad to see her brother
when he came for her, she almost screamed out,
" Oh ! no,—I hope he won't come ! If he does, I
shall be ready to creep into a bottle !" On seeing
a mouse, she said that they used often to have dor-
mice which they called the *seven sleepers.* We
kept two young hedgehogs in a box in the kitchen
to clear us of blackclocks. They only came out in
the evening. On first seeing one of them she appeared quite delighted, as if she had met with
an old acquaintance ; she snatched it up in her
hand, exclaiming, " Oh, you old gentleman ; but I'll
make you both whistle and sing !" On being asked
how she would do that, she said by squeezing his
toes. The mother of one of the servants was stop-
ping with us, to whom Clara became much attached.
" Well, Clara," she said, " when you come into the

neighbourhood where I live, you'll be sure and call to see me." "Oh! yes! I'm sure I will; for you know Mrs. T., that though mountains and valleys cannot come together,—distant friends can."

With two of my daughters she soon became a favourite; always humble and respectful, but when told to sit down, either to converse, to be instructed, or to teach them the Gypsy language, she never appeared neither awkward or timid. She expressed herself in very proper language, with a little of a foreign tone and manner, pronouncing the T, de. She made use of no provincialisms. The circuit which she had been accustomed to take, was very extensive, from the northern parts of Yorkshire, to Sussex, &c. She soon learned her letters, and made them very well on a slate, but did not appear ready at combining them into words. Her comprehension, on any subject proposed, appeared to be very quick and clear, and her feelings acute. On the subject of religion, she knew but little. In a short conversation which I had with her respecting God, she was much affected. She knew that there was a God, but had not, till she came to us, been used to pray, but said that she did now, every night and morning, and always would. She said, with tears, that she was sure she loved God, and felt that He loved her. She went with the servants to church, she had frequently been in one, but never where there was an organ, with that she was much pleased. The child behaved so well, and appeared to be so happy and thankful, that I concluded to keep her at least for some time longer. On telling her so, and asking if she thought her brother

would let her stay, she said that she was sure that
they both would be very glad, and very much obliged to me.

The brother came at the time fixed, and both
surprised and grieved me, by declaring that he
should be obliged to take Clara with him. He expressed his obligations as strongly as language
could do, indeed, I had difficulty in restraining him
from going down on his knees to me ; still he said
that though he knew that it would be greatly to the
advantage of both himself and his sister for her
to stay, yet, that his wife and one child were so ill
that he had been obliged to hire a woman to take
care of them, and could not possibly do without
Clara. We were all much concerned, as we wished
to qualify the girl for making a respectable servant,
and also to learn more from her of the manners and
language of the Gypsies. The brother on first seeing his sister had, I found, told her his intention of
taking her away. I sent for her into the room, she
had been in tears. I told her that as he was only
her brother, she was old enough to decide for herself whether to go with him or stay, and that she
should do as she herself determined. She said at
once, without hesitation, that, as they wanted her,
she would wish to go. I told her that she judged
very properly, and that we should always be glad
to see her. I strongly suspected that the man was,
however, deceiving me. I left home before them,
and in my way to the town, I met with the wife,
who said that she was as well as usual, and did not
wish for Clara's return.

I can only account for the man's conduct on the

supposition of his being acted upon by that Divine fiat which hath ordained the Gypsies to remain a distinct and *dispersed* people, till the fullness of the time for their re-assembling in their own country shall arrive. I had not much opportunity of conversation with the man, but as far as I had, it went fully to confirm the information given to me by Boswell, though he was not either so intelligent or personable a man as the latter.

During Clara's stay with us, my daughters endeavoured to obtain what information they could from her respecting the language spoken by the Gypsies. In some instances, she certainly was not so competent as others might have been to afford it. What they obtained, however, may probably suffice, in some degree, to gratify curiosity, and lead to some useful result. From the lists of words which have been obtained, and published, from Gypsies in different countries, it is ascertained that the language spoken by them all, has originally been the same. There is a little difference in the pronunciation, and consequently in the spelling; as might be expected, in many instances, they have several names for the same thing. In every country it is probable that they substitute words from the language of that country, wherever they are at a loss for words in their own, or whenever they find them readier or better. The following list of words which my daughters obtained from their interesting visitor, though probably in many respects imperfect, may be found interesting. Had they been at all aware that her stay would have been so short, they would have enabled themselves to have given a much fuller and clearer account of the language, than they have been able to do. Much as I am sure that poor Clara was attached to us, and much as I am assured that it was her wish, and intention, to see us whenever she could, as she faithfully promised to do, we have never, in the course of four years, either seen or heard any of or thing from her. I doubt not but that the family have since purposely kept away from the district. Nothing, I think, can account for the conduct of the party in this instance, but that intuitive, though perhaps unconscious, bias of the mind, which keeps the Gypsies, as ordained, a distinct and vagrant people.

The following is the list already referred to :—

* Duvvel	God.
Congling...:..............	Church.
Ca-ha	House.
Tanya	Tent.
† Granza	Barn.
Burrouco	Shop.
Starrapan.................	Prison.
Kichimmo	Alehouse.
Waggaulus	Fair.
Gav....	Town.
Wudda............	Door.
Stigga	Gate.
Drum	Road.
Shello....	Well.

* Greek, (obsolete) Dis.—Latin, Deus.—Italian, Dio.—French, Dieu.

† Italian, Granogo.—French, Grange.

Shammit	Chain.
Wuddress	Bed.
Roi	Spoon.
Churee	Knife.
Pusramangara	Fork.
Currio	Earthen vessel.
Chivya	Tongs.
Mumlee	Candle.
Duddramangru	Lanthern.
Poof	The Earth.
Chick	
Pofe	Field.
Wesh	Wood.
Pan	River.
Ruk	Tree.
Mush	Man
Romino	Gypsey.
Mannishee	Woman.
Chau	Boy.
Chi	Girl.
Ticcino	Baby.
Dad	Father.
Di	Mother.
Pal	Brother.
Pen	Sister.
Coc	Uncle.
Bibbi	Aunt.
Pourouchau	*Grandchild.
Galway	Girl.

* For Grandfather, the Gipsies say, Puradad; for Grandmother, Poureedi; old Father, old Mother. Thus Pourouchau must signify child of age.

Arai	Gentleman.
Araunah	Lady.
Derai	Master.
Sherrou	Head.
Mush	Arm.
Wast	Hand.
Herro	Leg.
Pero	Foot.
Wangisha	Finger.
Yoc	*Eye.
Noc	Nose.
Chunga	Lips.
Chiv	Tongue.
Darya	Teeth.
See	Heart.
Cam	Ear.
Muy	Mouth.
Balla	Hair.
Chucca	Coat.
Shubbus	Gown.
Staddee	Bonnet.
Mushi-staddee	Hat.
Plashta	Cloak.
Huffo	Cap.
Panuigasha	Handkerchief.
Shoducca	Apron.
Truppa	Stays.
Chaca	Shoes.
Craton	Button.
Caningarou	Ear-ring.
Mericla	Necklace.

* Latin, Oculus.—Italian, Occhio.

Coppa	Blanket.
Catse	Scissors.
Souve	Needle.
Spinga	*Pin.
Butsee	Work.
Kell	Play.
Tav	Thread.
Killin	Dance.
Giv	Song.
Bosshimangree	Fiddle.
Lill	Book.
Chinnamasngree	Letter.
Cheris	Time.
Hapristicheris	Dinner-time.
Wudrusticheris	Bed-time.
Besh	Year.
Divvus	†Day.
Sola	Morning.
Ratee	Night.
Dud	Light.
Pratness	Darkness.
Yog	Fire.
Tow	Smoke.
Yoggramangee	Gun.
Bars	Ship.
Baringro	Sailor.
Wardo	Cart.
Chuckinee	Whip.
Mea	Mile.

* French, Epingle.
† Latin, Dies.—Italian, Di.—Divum, in Latin, is day-light.

Pash	Half.
Gruvnee	Beast.
Gry	Horse.
Gruvvenee	Cow.
Moyla	Ass.
Bachico	Sheep.
Juckal	Dog.
Caningo	Hare.
Shusho	Rabbit.
Bolo	Pig.
Hotchawitcha	Hedgehog.
Chericlo	Bird.
Pibblerannee	Turkey.
Pappin	Goose.
Retza	Duck.
Cannee	Hen.
Bashuo	Cock.
Poree	Feather.
Matcho	Fish.
Bouro	Snail.
Sap	Snake.
Cass	Hay.
Puss	Straw.
Giv	Corn.
Pono	Flour.
Moro	Loaf.
Mariclee	Cake.
Zud	Milk.
Smentinno	Cream.
Frill	Butter.
Yoro	Egg.
Pisha	Honey.

Gudlam	Sugar.
Muttramangaree	Tea.
Povingra	Potatoes.
Mass	Meat.
Pomya	*Apple.
Lun	Salt.
Livin	Ale.
Tattipani	Brandy.
Wallin	Bottle.
Canauvo	Turnip.
Shoc	Cabbage.
Sappin	†Soap.
Luvoo	Money.
Cutta	Guinea.
Gurrishtee	Shilling.
Bissha	Rain.
Gudlee	Noise.
Chinnamangree ‡	Hatchet.
Cosshtee	Stick.
Bar	Stone.
Gunno	Bag.
Sa	Laugh.
Suttee	Sleep.
Tatchapee	Truth.
Rouzha	Flower.
Ou	I.
Tut	Thou.
Mande	Me.

* Latin, Pomus.—Italian, Pomo.—French, Pomme.
† Latin, Sapo.—Italian, Sapone.—French, Savon.
‡ Many of these words have the termination mangree, perhaps in all instances of similar signification.

Yeck	One.
Due	*Two.
Trin	†Three.
Pange	Four.
Disk	Five.
Bitta...........................	Small.
Borum.........	Large.
Podo	Full.
Cushto	Good.
Arincina	Pretty.
Rincana	Handsome.
Tuggonso	Sorry.
Acola	Black.
Apono	White.
Allullo	Red.
Tatto	Hot
Skil	Cold.
Yaw	To walk.
Nash...........................	Run.
Besh	Sit.
Sofe	Lie.
Hatchaparai...................	Rise.
Kista	Ride.
Kell	Dance.
Jaungkell	Play.
Hav	Come.
Jodra	Enter.
Bacca	Bacca.

* Greek, Duo; Latin, Duo; Italian, Duc; French, Deux.

† Greek, Treis; Latin, Tres; Italian Tre; French, Trois.

Giv	Sing.
Boshree	Fiddle.
Wottogudlee	Shout.
Sai	Laugh.
Burwin	Weep.
Mulloo	Die.
Choa	Steal.
Man	Kill.
Chinger	Quarrel.
Cooa	Fight.
Del	Strike.
Haw	Hate.
Com	Love.
Dic	See.
Shoon	Hear.
Sung	Smell.
Bucclo	Hunger.
Han	Eat.
Pe	Drink.
Cerroo	Boil.
Ceddo	Roast.
Hotcha	Burn.
Tofe	Smoke.
Shucco	Dry.
Bissha	Rain.
Clisn	Lock.
Pirronit	Open.
Podo	Fill.
Chivitadra*a*	Put in.
Sellitaree *a*	Take out.
Kell	Reach.
Kellitapra *a*	Wrap up.

Chivvitaley a...............	} Throw down.
Wusra	
Sellitapra a...	Take up.
Pertaley...............	Fall.
Wusrit	Throw.
Biggerit	Carry.
Delman	Ask.
Del	Give.
Sel	Take away.
Latcht.......	Find.
Parrac......................	Thank.
Kin	Buy.
Bikkin....................	Sell.
Ruddee	Dress.
Auriggu	Undress.
Pan ....'......	Tie.
Chinglet	Tear.
Chivan...............'........	Put on.
Chinnet	Cut.
Sivit........................	Sew.
Hecco	Haste.
Jin.	Know.
Nafflee	Be ill.

One word, distinguished by no inflexions, is all that the Gypsies use to form the moods and tenses of a verb. Though they retain in their language

---

   * In the words marked a, terminating in dra, leg, and ee, the Gypsy-girl laid a particular emphasis on the last syllable. Perhaps they are two words as in English, but we did not ask the question.

the pronouns, ou I ; tŭt, thou : mande, me ; they appear to prefer the English ones, and in other cases to supply, from necessity, the deficiencies of their language by English words :—

I dell	I give.
I dell yeyeok (a good while since)..........................	I gave.
I will dell.....................	I will give.
Dell	Give.
I may dell	I may give.
I might dell	I might give.
To dell	To give.

As there are no particular inflexions for particular parts of speech, the same word occurs both as substantive and verb, as giv, song ; to giv, to sing ; but not always; killin, dance ; to kell, to dance.

Though these two instances are the only ones which has happened to come under my own immediate observation, I am happy to be able to bring forward others equally creditable to the Gypsy character, which I have had the pleasure of meeting with lately. They are contained in a small work, entitled " *The Gypsies,*" written by a clergyman of the Church of England. They will, I am sure, be read with interest, and cannot fail to produce considerable impressions in favour of that calumniated race of human beings, the Gypsies. They will, I trust, likewise dispose the hearts of many to encourage any benevolent scheme which may be proposed, likely

to conduce to the real benefit of so large a class of
necessitous and confiding strangers.   These are the
kind of facts which are wanted to remove the prejudices which have for centuries been entertained
against these wandering outcasts.   They are facts
which cannot fail of success in their appeal, both to
the heart and to the understanding of those who
read them :—

" A journey to see a friend about two years back,
brought me into contact with the Gypsies.   It
was late in the year, and the winds had nearly stripped the trees of their umber foliage : here and there
were seen, yet in verdure, the lower branches of the
sturdy oak ; while the gloomy yew, frowning with
age, frequently presented itself as if to call the
traveller's attention to the age, and men, and times
which were past.   My road lay partly through a
hilly picturesque country, chequered with farms,
hamlets, and villas, and partly through a winding
wood.   By the time I arrived at the wood, the sun
was sinking below the horizon, and the evening
shadows were investing nature,   Meditation, however, on the varied surrounding scenery occupied
my mind, and beguiled the way.   While thus engaged, my musings were all on a sudden inter-
rupted : I had just reached a declivity near the ex-
tremity of the wood, when a child suddenly crossed
the road, and so near to me, that it narrowly
escaped being trampled on by my pony ; the little
creature, unconscious of its danger or deliverance
looked up upon me, and innocently smiled. At first
I was ready to wonder from whence it had come ;

but its swarthy face, its black hair and eyes, plainly bespoke its family and its people. My conjectures were not incorrect; for turning myself, I discovered on a grassy bank, half concealed by some spreading trees, an encampment of Gypsies.

" Here a subject presented itself for the investigation of the philosopher, and for the active benevolence of the Christian; here I might have stopped and brought into action my Christian charity, by giving to those perishing outcasts some salutary advice respecting both worlds. I might have directed them to the source of peace here, and to the source of blessedness and glory hereafter; but I did neither. I felt desirous of hastening to my journey's end before the darkness of night had obscured my path. Thus, to avoid a little personal inconvenience, how often do we neglect the opportunity heaven designs to put into our hands, for great and virtuous deeds! But this little adventure was of consequence, inasmuch as it led to an acquaintance with this people, and to a desire for their welfare.

" On my arrival at my friend's, among other things, the Gypsies in their encampment in the wood became the subject of our conversation. It would have been interesting to us to have made out their true origin, and to have traced them from it through their different gradations to their present state; but as conjectures only could be given on that head, our minds were directed to their moral state. I was satisfied that they were the children of Adam, under the curse of sin, and without hope and without God in the world.   The most melancholy part of the picture, however, was the ignorance in which the apathy of Christians had so long suffered them to lie, and the barrier which their wandering habits presented, to prevent regular and constant instruction.

*   *   *   *

"The morning of the next day presented me with the opportunity which I had the evening before lost and regretted.   The Gypsies whom I had seen encamped in the wood, were passing by the door of my friend's house, and in that direction which I myself had that morning to go on a visit to another friend.   Providence in this case seemed to be propitious to my wishes, and to invite me to my purpose.

"In a short time, I mounted my pony, and overtook them.   They were scattered in their march like a flock of sheep: the main body with the baggage at some distance in front, some females and children in detached groups behind.   I thought, here is an opportunity of instructing these wanderers; I can catechise them and converse with them as I ride along.

"I immediately joined the rear-guard; it was composed of a female, apparently about eighteen years of age, dressed in a tidy and neat manner, with a sweet baby at her back: her features were particularly dark and handsome, with fine expressive black eyes.

"I introduced myself by some observations on

the manners of a Gypsy life, and then turned the conversation on religion. I soon found, to my surprise, that the Gypsy female possessed a very correct knowledge of the subject. Her answers were particularly satisfactory and pleasing; they discovered a mind and language far above her station. Indeed, her whole deportment and appearance indicated something superior.

" ' How,' I said, ' did you obtain this knowledge of religion?' ' Sir,' she answered, ' in the depth of winter, the men folks only travel ; the women and children belonging to the family and party, always live in the town of C——. In those seasons, I have gone with some of our relations, who live there, who are religious people, to the worship of God ; in that way I have learned these things.' This I could readily believe ; it at once explained the matter, and was a practical comment on the text which says, ' The entrance of thy words giveth light; it giveth understanding unto the simple.' After giving her some suitable advice, and with it my benediction, I left her, but not without hopeful expectations that seeds of grace were sown in her heart. May the beams of heaven foster them, thou wanderer, and amid all the inclemencies to which thou art exposed, cause thee to flourish as a tree of righteousness! I will not fail to pray for thee, thou lovely wandering Gypsy female, thou young pilgrim! that the God who has instructed thee, and whom thou worshippest may ever be thy protector, friend, and guide. Mayest thou, although dark, be comely in his sight, and be found among his chosen ones in the day when he maketh up his jewels !'

"The next that I overtook were the grandmother and several of her grand-children. She was pleased at my noticing her, and answered my inquiries with modesty and propriety. She corroborated what her daughter had said; and, in her answers discovered not only an acquaintance with the general truths of the Gospel, but also a feeling sense of their importance. ' I love to go to church, and do, Sir, now, when I can ; but do not always meet with the right doctrines : my prayers I offer up night and morning under the hedge. I hope God Almighty hears my prayers.' I assured her that He did, and that sincere prayer was acceptable to him any where : equally under the hedge, as in the parlour or in the church. I left her with my instructions, and rode forward to overtake the main body. Here were men and boys, children and asses, horses and carts, pack and package.

"My salutation was received with civility. Trade was bad, they informed me ; for they were sellers of earthern pans and pots. The subject of religion was easily introduced ; and to my question, what the captain of the gang himself knew of these things ?—he frankly confessed his sin :—he feelingly said, ' Sir, I know a great deal more than I practice. I have heard of these things before, and confess to you how sensible I feel of my neglect of what I knew to be my duty.' He made the whole of this declaration with so much seeming sensibi-

lity of heart, that I was constrained to credit his
testimony. This gave me a fine opportunity of in-
troducing my favourite subject. The conversation
soon became very interesting, and the young men
and the boys were all attention; even the children
in the packs on the asses listened with evident interest, while I discoursed on the state of man
through sin, the necessity of repentance, and of
faith in our Lord Jesus Christ.

"I now inquired whether any one among them
could read. An interesting young man, whose
countenance bespoke great simplicity and sincerity,
was pointed out to me. 'He,' they said, 'can read
a little.' 'How much can he read?' 'He can
read a chapter, Sir.' This was the point I wanted
to ascertain. 'Have you any books?' 'A few religious books among the packages.' I was happy
of course to hear this. These little tracts were
silent missionaries, and always at hand to point out
some important duty. It is impossible to say how
much these little books might have contributed towards the civilization and moral improvement of
these wandering outcasts; doubtless they had their
share in the good work.

"I had contemplated, however, a better book for
them. I had conceived the design of giving them
a Bible. I thought, what an interesting companion
in their travels would a Bible prove! What light
and blessedness might it cast in their mortal pil-
grimage; no boon to equal that to man, no boon
to equal that to them! 'If I give you a Bible will
you esteem it? Would you solemnly promise to

read it?' 'Yes, we will, Sir,—we will take the
greatest care of it : it shall ever be our instructor :
we will listen to it night and morning.'

*   *   *   *

" It was to me also a subject of high gratification to find these poor Gypsies in possession of so
much moral and religious information, and so desirous of instruction, so willing to hear the words
of life.

" I now arrived at my friend's,—almost my first
inquiry was for a Bible. My friend, who was the
secretary of a Bible Association, was able to supply my wishes. I had hardly mentioned the circumstance, when a knock was heard at the door,
' Two Gypsies, Sir, come for a Bible.' On my going out, I found in the hall the young man who
could read, and a younger brother, a fine boy about
fourteen years of age. The countenances were
very animated and expressive ; there seemed already to have been a ray of heavenly brightness
resting upon them ; and while I gave them a charge
how to read the sacred gift, they were much affected : the boy in particular listened with eager
attention, fixing his eyes first on me, then on the
Bible. After I had inscribed their name on the
title page, they departed with my blessing ; and,
what is better, with the blessing of God. Doubtless that God, who has promised that his word shall
not return void, will own the gift to these wanderers
from his fold. I cannot but believe that some fruits
of British Christian benevolence and charity to all
nations will spring up to the glory and honour of

God among the despised, scattered, and peeled
Gypsies. This book of God may not only be the
source of light, of peace, of comfort, and joy to
this people in their various journeys and travels
through this mortal life; but it may shed a beam
of glory on their last earthly footsteps; it may
open a sacred vista to a country where mortal degradations, toil and wandering shall for ever cease;
and where Gypsies, beggars, and kings, who are
washed in the blood of the Lamb, shall sit down
together. It may raise these wanderers to the
fruition of everlasting glory in the kingdom of
heaven. In such a faith will I conclude the first
part of my narrative. 'Blessed be the Lord God,
and the God of Israel, who only doeth wondrous
things, and blessed be his glorious name for ever;
and let the whole earth be filled with his glory.
Amen and Amen.'

* * * * *

"Early in the spring of the present year, I went
to spend a week with some dear friends, in the
same part of the country, where before I had met
with the group of Gypsies mentioned in my last
narrative.

"The day after my arrival, I rode over to call on
my friend, the secretary of the Bible Association,
already referred to in my narrative.

"When I had proceeded about half way, turning
my head, I observed, on my right hand, in a lane
leading from S****w-wood to a hamlet, a Gypsy
encampment. The waste ground was occupied with
tents and packages; their horses and their asses

feeding by their side, while a fire from collected broken branches, ever and anon sent forth, in many curling columns, the fumid exhalation, and filled the air with its woody odour.

" Instantly I turned my horse, and rode up to reconnoitre the camp. Near the packages and tents, I found several of the swarthy race of Ham, some recumbent, others standing. A group of nearly naked children were playing round a tub. The only persons who at that time were there, besides the children, were some interesting young women. The chief of the party, consisting of two men and several women, were absent on a trading expedition to the neighbouring towns and villages.

· " On my approach to the camp, the Gypsy girls rose up, and, in a modest and respectful manner, answered my questions; while the little swarthy group of children gathered round me.

" To one of these girls I said, ' How is it that you bear such a wandering and exposed life?' In reply, she said, · ' Sir, it is use ; use is second nature.' But have you any religion ? Do you think about God, about judgment, and eternity ? Do you know how to pray?' She answered, 'I say my prayers, Sir, night and morning.' I then said, can any of your people read ?' ' Yes, Sir,' she replied, ' one of our women that is not here can read very well.' ' Have you a Bible among you!' ' No, Sir.' 'Would you like some little books?' ' We should be very thankful for any, Sir.'

· " After some religious instruction, adapted more immediately to their case, I told them that I would

endeavour to call on them again as I came back.
I then left them to pursue my way.

"As I rode along, my mind was much interested
and affected with the moral degradation and
wretchedness of this lost people. They seemed
to cry in my ears, 'No man careth for my soul.' I
thought, How is it Christians are every where zea-
lous for the conversion of the heathen in foreign
lands, but these poor dying heathen at home, and
at our very doors, are left to perish in ignorance,
wretchedness, and guilt? The more I revolved the
subject in my mind, the more was I convinced of
the duty of Christians to attempt means for their
instruction and conversion, and the more was
I ashamed for their long neglect. I resolved instantly myself to do something for them, although
it should be but little ; and among other things, I
determined to ascertain their ability to read, and
their disposition to receive the Bible. On my arrival at my friend's, I made him acquainted with
my second Gypsy adventure, and with my intention of giving them some suitable tracts, and with
them a Bible. To this he cordially assented, and
again furnished me with a Bible and some tracts for
my mission. My plan, I told him, was not to give
the Bible on my return, but to request the whole of
the tribe to be collected together in the evening,
about seven o'clock, then to ride over, and after ex-
plaining to them the value and use of the sacred
boon, to deposit it with them, with solemn prayer.

"On my return, the different branches of this
Gypsy family had assembled together. They had

got back from their trading expedition, and were
waiting in expectation of my coming.   On my
riding up to the encampment, I was met by two
men, who came up to greet me : one of them had a
very open and interesting countenance ; the features of the others were dark and suspicious : they
were both evidently of Gypsy origin.   I asked
them kindly of their name, of their welfare, and of
their trade.   They informed me that their name
was Bosvile ; that they were what was called Bosvile's gang ; they said they carried on three trades,
they were knife-grinders, chair-bottomers, and
china-menders ; that they had not been very successful that day, but that they often were, and when
they had a good day, it made up for a bad one.
This, I thought, is pleasing ; it shews, at any rate,
a disposition among these wanderers to industry
and contentment, and reads to many an useful
lesson.

" The women and children were now collected
around me.   I inquired who among them could
read.   Captain Bosvile, for so I called him, answered me, ' My wife, Sir, can read any thing in
English.'   I was glad at the circumstance, and now
asked them whether they had any books.   Bosvile,
on this, went to a package, and brought me forth
his stock, a fragment of an old Testament, and an
old Spelling Book.   ' And what do you do with
the Spelling Book ?' said I.   ' My wife,' replied
Bosvile, ' with that, when she has time, teaches the
children their letters.'

" The fact of a part of the Scriptures being

found with a Gypsy tribe, and of a Gypsy woman being able to read, and teaching the children to read, was to me a most singular thing; it impressed me with a better idea of Gypsies than before I had entertained, and could not fail of calling forth my approbation. I then distributed among them my little messengers of mercy, particularly prayers for every day in the week, and short sermons; these I solemnly charged them to read.

" My little books were received with great eagerness and thankfulness. I now said, " I have entertained some thoughts of giving you a Bible; how would it be received?' 'We will be very thankful, we will be very thankful for it,' was the reply. Indeed, their countenances bespoke the interest which the proposal had excited in their minds, a book which few of them had ever seen, and fewer understood. I now pointed to the Bible in my pocket, and told them, that since it was such a holy and blessed book, it must not be given in an indifferent and common way, and asked, if I were to ride over in the evening to give it them, and to explain to them its use, would they be altogether to hear me? ' Yes, yes,' was replied from various quarters. I then appointed seven o'clock for the purpose, and after some other conversation, rode to T****.

"It may be supposed, that the state of these Gypsies had excited in my mind as much interest as my book and visit had excited in their minds; particularly when I found in them such modesty

of deportment and eagerness of soul after instruction; certainly they appeared a people whose
hearts the Lord had prepared for the reception of
his word.

"At the hour appointed, I put on my coat, put
the Bible in my pocket, mounted my pony, and
rode to the camp. The evening was particularly
fine. The sun, hidden behind some thick fleecy
clouds, had thrown around a mild and pleasing tint;
the birds every where singing their evening song,
the ploughman whistling o'er the lea, and nature,
after the labours of the day, preparing for her
wonted rest. It was fit time for meditation, for
prayer, and for praise. Such an evening, perhaps,
as that which led the patriarch of old to meditation,
when he lifted up his eyes and saw the returning
servants of his father, bringing on their camels the
fair Rebecca and her nurse.

"As I drew near to their camp, I began to re-
volve in my mind the best way of making them acquainted with the most essential doctrines contained
in the book I was about to give them, and of their
importance. I thought the opportunities of instruction to these poor Gypsies are so few and partial, and their minds so enveloped in sin and unbelief, something must now be done for them, at least
some attempt must be made to discover to them
their darkness, and direct them to the true light;
and that in a manner most calculated to strike their
minds.

"On my arrival, I found that I had been long
expected. The men, however, were not there;

they were gone to water a horse, which had just come from work, and which they had lent all the day to a farmer.   An express was now sent off for them: a tawny girl ran with great speed barefooted, and brought them to the camp. I now dismounted from my horse, and gave it, with my stick, to the care of one of the men.   The family was formed into a sort of circle around some pale embers of a dying fire; some of them were sitting cross-legged on the grass, others standing.   I placed myself so as to have the women and children chiefly before me.   The woman who could read I seated opposite on the tub, which, in the morning, had been occupied by the children; the men, the tents, my pony and the package to the right; the horses and asses belonging to the tribe were quietly grazing at a short distance in the lane. All was solemn stillness: all was attention and expectation.

"Now, I took from my pocket the Bible; and instantly the eyes of the whole company were fixed upon it. 'This book,' I said, 'which I bring you, is the book of God; it is sent from heaven to make poor, miserable, and dying men happy.'

"I spoke at first on God: on creation; how God created man upright: how he was once happy in Paradise: the way in which he sinned and broke the law of his Maker, and became guilty, polluted, and exposed to death and hell: how to save men from this dreadful state, God devised a plan of mercy; He sent his word, the scriptures of truth, which show unto us the way of salvation through his Son.   This was something of the outline of my lecture ; but I added the responsibility of men to read the book, to seek to understand it.   I solemnly charged them, by the sacred book itself, by the account which they, at the day of judgment, must give to God for it, to make the most sacred and constant use of it by reading it together daily in their camp.

" In the course of my discourse I stopped. I said, 'Now do you understand what I say?'   Captain Bosville's wife replied, 'We understand you, Sir, but we have not the same words which you have.' In conclusion, I spoke of the coming judgment, when they and all men must stand and be judged at the rghteous bar of God.

" The Bible was then delivered to the care of the Captain of the gang, and of his wife, the woman who could read.

" Now, I said, let us all kneel down on the grass, and let us pray for God's blessing, with this holy book.   Instantly a female brought from her tent a carpet, and spread it before me on the grass to kneel upon.   We then all kneeled down, and I prayed that the eyes of these miserable outcasts of society might be enlightened, to discover the exceeding sinfulness of sin, and the blessedness of a Saviour; that the sacred book given them, through the influence of the Holy Ghost, might lead them into the way of righteousness, and finally bring them to everlasting life.

" It was a solemn time,—not a breath to be heard ! save the rustling of the trees, which were agitated by the evening breeze, and the sweet melody of the songsters of the grove, who were offering to Heaven their expression of praise for the mercies of the day. Their song, at this time, seemed to sound more melodious, as if they had listened and approved the holy duties in which we had been engaged ; but whether or not, Heaven approved, and the recording angel made mention of it before the throne of God.

"When we arose from our knees, gratitude was seen in every countenance, and expressed by every tongue. 'God bless you, Sir, thank you, Sir,' echoed throughout the camp.

"I then inquired when they would leave that spot. I was answered, 'On the Friday.' l said, that as I should be at liberty the next evening, I would again ride over, if they would get together at the same hour. The proposal was received with great joy.

"I now shook hands with my swarthy congregation : men, women, girls, and children all pressed around me to thank me, and to bid me good bye. I mounted my pony and rode away, followed with their blessings. Just at that moment, the sun which before had been hidden with clouds, broke forth and shed his last setting beams with peculiar splendour. I said, 'Surely here is an omen of the shining of the sun of righteousness on this fallen people, although the day is far spent, and the night is at hand. Yet, in that interval, may the bright and healing beams of his immortal glory break on their hearts : even so Amen ; come Lord Jesus.

" I thought here, again, I have had proof of the disposition of poor Gypsies to receive moral and religious instruction. Never did I speak to a more attentive con gregation : never did a congregation appear more interested. May God bless the feeble effort, and raise up from this peeled nation a seed to serve Him, a people to glorify his name for ever in the kingdom of Heaven.

*   *   *   *   *

" These preliminary arrangements being made, I set out as on the preceding evening, taking with me my pocket Bible. Before, however, I had got out of the town, I was met by my dear G——, from B——: he had just come over, and had on the road passed the Gypsy encampment. He brought me the news of a fresh arrival : another party or family of Gypsies had just got to the ground, as he came up. These were also called Bosviles, and were what the other party termed their aunts. They had no sooner reached the spot, than they were informed of my expected visit : instantly their asses were unloaded, and their tents pitched : all was bustle and hurry to get ready by the time I came. Some of the females, I was told, were at their toilet ; and all of them arraying themselves in their gala dresses.

" I was much pleased, it may be supposed, to hear of these circumstances, as it gave me an unexpected opportunity of addressing a much larger congregation of these outcasts of society, and of knowing more of their disposition to the truth.

" Before I arrived at the camp, I was met by Captain Bosvile and his friend; they came out to meet me, and to bid me welcome. I shook hands with them, asked how they did, and talked of their relatives that had just come. They then conducted me to the camp. Here I was met by all my old friends, men, women, and children; they all gathered with welcome greetings around me. I was much struck with the pastoral simplicity, the civility, and etiquette of my reception. Never was a king received with a more hearty welcome, or with greater attention and respect. It certainly evidenced something of the paternal manners, something of the customs which they had derived from the ancient usages of their forefathers.

" I now dismounted my pony, and gave it, as before, to the care of one of the Bosviles. I was then introduced to the strangers, who had just arrived. On looking about me, I could easily discern that my coming was anticipated; the utmost order, cleanliness, and quiet prevailed throughout the camp: every thing appeared in its proper place, and every one appeared in their best attire. One of the young females had braided her long black hair, and very tastefully twisted it over her forehead. The aunts, however, were the most conspicuous : they were fine looking young females, with true Gypsy features, and dressed in the highest order of Gypsy fashion. One of them wore a loose dress of large printed cotton, with rolling collar, with deep flounce, and apron to match. The men, too, I observed, were in best trim : shaved, and clean, and neat. I hardly could have supposed a tribe of Gypsies capable of exhibiting such a picture of order, neatness, and respectability.

"I could not but feel great pleasure in the contemplation of this mark of civilization, and of respect for the Gospel. I thought if my accidental visit has created this manifest interest and attention, what would not the constant and persevering preaching of the Gospel do by a regular ministry? From this interesting group might many arise, and shine among the church of the redeemed on earth, and among the church of the first-born, as the stars for ever and ever in heaven.

"My arrangement of my congregation was much the same as on the preceding evening. The blue heavens formed the roof of our sanctuary, the green grass was our floor, the wide spreading oaks waved gently in the air ; and the evening sun was reclining in the western sky ; the lark was carolling his evening lay, and the thrush and the blackbird responding their songs in the wood. The God of nature, the God of glory, and the God of grace, was present. He could deign to meet the Patriarchs of old when worshipping amidst groves, and woods, and fields, and He in his mercy deigned to meet with us. The promise of Messiah made for us was claimed.

"The only alteration which I made, was in the seating before me on the tub occupied the last evening by the Captain's wife, the aged grandmother of

the aunts, a feeble old woman, bearing on her
shoulders nearly a century of years. My congregation together could not have consisted of much
less than thirty persons.

"In commencing my discourse with them, I
took out my little Bible from my pocket, and referred to the Bible I had given them the last evening. I said, as before, I brought you the best of
books; so now I come to tell you of the best of
persons—the chief character spoken of in that
book. My subject led me to speak of Christ in
his birth, in his ministry, in his death, and in his
passion, in his grace and in his glory, in his second
coming in the clouds of heaven to judge the world
in righteousness. I spoke also of death, and of
immortality of the soul.

"I had not proceeded far in my lecture before
my congregation was augmented. Several farmers
and passengers, some on horseback, others on foot,
attracted by my voice and the novelty of our pastoral devotion, came near us and listened to my discourse. At first the singularity of the thing pro-
voked a smile; but soon the word gained access to
their hearts, and the greatest seriousness was maintained; it may be strictly said, that, 'Those who
came to laugh remained to pray.'

"Before I concluded my address, I said, 'It
may seem to some of you singular, that a stranger
should interest himself on your behalf in the way
I have done; and it might be expected that I
should give some reasons for so doing. My chief
reason is a sense of duty: Gypsies might have long

been neglected, and left to perish in their sins ; but Gypsies have souls equally precious as others, and of equal price in sight of God.   Who, I said, cares for the souls of Gypsies ?   Who uses means for their instruction in righteousness ?   Yet must it be equally our duty to care for them, and endeavour their conversion and happiness, as to plan societies, obtain subscriptions, and send out missionaries to the heathen '

*   *   *   *   *

"I now proposed to take leave of my swarthy flock ; but it was not without feelings of attachment on both sides.   I had observed several of them much affected under my discourse, and now they manifested it more openly.   As I shook hands with them, I said, · You see I did not come among you to give you any money.   I considered religious instruction of the most value ; therefore, I have endeavoured to impart it.'   'Sir, replied several, 'we did not want your money ; your instruction is better to us than money, and we thank you for coming.'   The camp now resounded with 'Thank you, Sir ; God bless you, Sir.'   Every countenance was animated, and every heart seemed to beat.   The young branches of the family seemed to consider some great honour and blessing conferred upon them.

"As I mounted my pony to come away, I observed one of the females, a fine young woman, about twenty-five years of age, the same that brought the carpet from the package, and spread it on the grass for me to kneel upon, to retire from the rest·

She walked slowly near to the hedge, and appeared evidently much distressed. Her expressive eyes were lifted up to heaven, while the big tears rolling down her cheeks were wiped away with her long black tresses. I thought, here surely are some of the first fruits. Thus did the woman, who was a sinner, weep, and with her hair wipe away her tears from the feet of her Saviour. May those tears be as acceptable to God; may the same Redeemer bid her go in peace!

"My friends who had come to the camp, as strangers passing by, now mingled with the Gypsies, and asked them many questions on the subject of my visiting them. Their answers were such as shewed them their interest in the subjects I had set before them. The conduct of the weeping female, who had gone from the company to a private part of the camp, particularly attracted their notice. The tears ran fast from her eyes. They asked her the reason of her sorrow. She at first could hardly speak. At length she exclaimed, ' O, I am a sinner!' Then, lifting up her eyes to heaven, she wept aloud, and wiped away the falling tears with the hair of her head. ' But did you not know that before? We are all sinners. What have you done to cause you so much distress?' She made no reply, but shook her head and wept. Just at that spot, another female Gypsy, an elderly woman, had come and sat herself down on some packages. She immediately replied, ' O, she may well weep, she is such a sinner; I know what distresses her; she has been such a bad child to her father and mother;

G

she has been bad also to her aunts ; she is a very bad sinner.   But as for me, I always put my trust in God, and He is always my friend ; and I always will put my trust in Him, and He will never forsake me.'   She spoke this with evident marks of self-righteousness, and laid great emphasis on her trusting in God, and God not forsaking her.   My friend had now an opportunity of shewing this Pharisaic Gypsy—for so she proved—how much she also was a sinner, and needed, equally with the weeping penitent, a Saviour.   This she at length acknowledged, and, with the other, was admonished to look for salvation alone to that Redeemer, who had been that evening set before her."

*   *   *   *

" From the whole of the narrative, much might be said by way of inference ; but as the limits of the publication are 'prescribed, only a few observations can be made.

" The first is, that in our own land, at our very doors, are found a heathen people in numbers, (as suggested in the survey,) not less than thirty-six thousand, living in a wild, scattered, and unsettled state, greatly sunk in ignorance, wretchedness, and error, useless to the government of the country, and in some instances, injurious to its morals.

" My second remark is, that although these people have been for centuries among us, no regular plan has yet been entered into for their amelioration and conversion ; that although societies have been established for the propagation of the Gospel in foreign parts, and for the promotion of Christian

knowledge at home, by Christians of different de-
nominations, yet is there no record of a society for
the express purpose of the moral improvement and
conversion of the Gypsies. I seem to stand amazed
at the fact. How is it that, in these latter days,
especially when the spirit of zeal rests upon the
churches, and when every Christian comes to the
help of the Lord against the mighty, that these
objects at our doors have been forgotten?"

It is a very remarkable circumstance that the
first notice which has reached us of the Gypsies, is
from almost all the States of Europe nearly about
the same time, viz. the early part of the fifteenth
century; beginning as early as 1400. How they
had found their way into each and all these numerous nations is no where clearly shewn. It is, however, equally remarkable, that in every one of them
they had then learned the language of the state in
which they were residing, and had even discovered
and taken advantage of the ignorance and failings
of the people and times. Superstition and belief
in the occult sciences were then general among all
classes of society. Of this propensity these newly
noticed people had in all countries had the sagacity
to discover and take advantage. Now, unless we
supposed that they had all dropped (as frogs and
snails are said at times to do,) at once, in all countries, from the clouds, possessed of all this knowledge, I do not see how we can avoid concluding
that they must have been for ages finding their way
to, and becoming acquainted with the several countries in which they were then for the first time

publicly noticed. In every country their appearance, their language, their habits, their manners, their employments were the same; all of them avoiding towns, and living in tents in secluded places in the country.

It is not pretended that the Gypsy character, even generally speaking, is not in many respects bad; it is, it must be so! but it is contended that it is not so vile as has been generally imagined, and that there are not any particular circumstances attaching either to themselves personally, or to their situation, which preclude the hope of rendering them Christians, and of affording them instruction, thereby contributing to the promotion of both their temporal and eternal welfare, and at the same time contributing to the general good of society. The attempt will require sound discussion as well as warm zeal. No attempt must be made to counteract habits which in them are nature. They must be permitted, if they desire it, to continue the same independent children of wild nature which they have always hitherto been. If better knowledge, and juster notions on religious subjects, work a change in that respect, we may conclude that the change will be for the best; if not, it may be that their present mode of living is the one appointed for them a little longer, till God's good time arrives for changing it.

As to what may be the way in which the attempt to enlighten their understandings, and to lead them to a knowledge of Christ, should be made, it is not, I think, difficult to determine. If the Gypsies can once be taught to read, they will in all probability become great readers. They have every opportunity, disposition, and inducement to render them such. They have much solitary time; they are a reflecting, thoughtful people, and they would find the ability to read, conducive to their interest as well as to their amusement. Let us only once succeed in convincing them that we seek to serve, and not to molest them, and we shall obtain their confidence; let us shew them favour, and we shall obtain their gratitude. They will then not only become communicative but tractable. Their dispersed state does certainly throw obstacles in the way of their general conversion and amelioration. All cannot, of course, be done at once; the great difficulty, however, will be in making a good beginning. As the plan is persevered in, and the good effects increase, the difficulties will in proportion be lessened. Every one gained will become more or less an assistant.

The following interesting extracts are principally taken from " The Gypsies' Advocate," by the Rev. JAMES CRABB :—

" Most of the Gypsies of this country are very punctual in paying their debts. All the shopkeepers, with whom they deal in these parts, have declared, that they are some of their best and most honest customers. For the payment of a debt which is owing to one of their own people, the time and place are appointed by them, and should the debtor disappoint the creditor, he is liable by their law of honour to pay double the amount he owes;

and he must pay it by personal servitude, if he cannot with money, if he wish to be considered by his friends honest and respectable.   They call this law *pizharris.*"

*   *   *   *

"It may naturally be expected that these inhabitants of the field and forest, the lane and the moor, are not without a knowledge of the medicinal qualities of certain herbs.   In all slight disorders they have recourse to these remedies, and frequently use the inner bark of the elm, 'star-in-the-earth,' pellitory-of-the-wall (pyrethrum), wormwood (absinthium), and parsley, (petroselinum).   And many of their old women are very useful in this way.   They are not generally subject to the numerous disorders and fevers common in large towns ; but in some instances they are visited with that dreadful scourge of the British nation, the typhus fever, which spreads through their little camp, and becomes fatal to some of its families.   The small-pox and measles are disorders they very much dread ; but they are not more disposed to rheumatic affections than those who live in houses.   It is a fact, however, that ought not to be passed over here, that when they leave their tents to settle in towns, they are generally ill for a time.   The children of one family that wintered with us in 1831 were nearly all attacked with fever that threatened their lives. This may be occasioned by their taking all at once to regular habits, and the renunciation of that exercise to which they have been so long accustomed, with some disposing qualities in their change of diet and the atmosphere of a thickly populated town.

"This people often live to a considerable age, many instances of which are well known. In his tent at Launton, Oxfordshire, died in the year 1830, more than a hundred years of age, James Smith, called by the public the King of the Gypsies. By his tribe he was looked up to with the greatest respect and veneration. His remains were followed to the grave by his widow, who is herself more than a hundred years old, and by many of his children, grand-children, great grand-children, and other relatives; and by several individuals of other tribes. At the funeral his widow tore her hair, uttered the most frantic exclamations, and begged to be allowed to throw herself on the coffin, that she might be buried with her husband."

* * * *

"The mutual attachment which subsists between the nominal husband and wife is so truly sincere that instances of infidelity, on either side, occur but seldom: and when otherwise, the parties are deemed very wicked by the Gypsies. They are known strictly to avoid all conversation of an unchaste kind in their camps, *except among the most degraded of them;* and instances of young females having children, before they pledge themselves to those they love, are rare. This purity of morals, among a people living as they do, speaks much in their favour.

"The anxiety of a Gypsy parent to preserve the purity of the morals of a daughter, is strongly

portrayed in the following fact. The author
wished to engage as a servant the daughter of a
Gypsy who was desirous of quitting her vagrant
life ; but her mother strongly objected for some
time ; and when pressed for the reason of such
objection, she named the danger she would be in
a town, far from a mother's eye. It would be well
if all others felt for their children as did this un-
lettered Gipsy. After having promised that the
morals of the child should be watched over, she
was confided to his care. And the author has
known a Gipsy parent correct with stripes a grown
daughter, for mentioning what a profligate person
had talked about.

" The following is an instance of conjugal attachment. A poor woman, whose eldest child is
now under the care of the Society for the improvement of the Gypsies, being near her confinement, came into the neighbourhood of Southampton, to be with her friends, who are reformed,
during the time. This not taking place so soon as
she expected, and having promised to meet her
husband at a distance on a certain day, he not
daring to show himself in Hampshire, she determined on going to him ; and having mounted her
donkey, set off with her little family. She had a
distance of nearly fifty miles to travel, and happily
reached the desired spot, where she met her husband before her confinement took place. The
good people of Warminster, near which place she
was, afforded her kind and needful assistance ; and
one well-disposed lady became godmother to the

babe, who was a fine little girl; the grateful
mother pledging that, at a proper age, she should
be given up to Christians to be educated.

"Before this woman left Southampton, referring
to many kind attentions shown her by the chari-
table of that place, she was heard to say, *Well!
I did not think any one would take such trouble
for me ?*"

* * * *

"It is a well-authenticated fact, that many persons pass for Gypsies who are not. Such persons
having done something to exclude them from society, join themselves to this people, and marrying
into their clans, become the means of leading them
into crimes they would not have thought of but
for their connection with such wicked people.
Coining money and forging notes, are, however,
crimes which cannot be *justly attributed to them.*
Indeed it has been too much the custom to impute
to them a great number of crimes of which they
either never were guilty, or which could only be
committed by an inconsiderable portion of their
race; and they have often suffered the penalty of
the law, when they have not in the least deserved
it. They have been talked of by the public, and
prosecuted by the authorities, as the perpetrators
of every vice and wickedness alike shocking to
civil and savage life. Nor is this to be wondered
at, living as they do, so remote from observation
and the walks of common life."

* * * *

"The author is not aware of any of them being

convicted of house-breaking, or highway robbery. Seldom are they guilty of sheep-stealing, or robbing hen-roosts.*   Nor can they be justly charged with stealing children ; this is the work of worthless beggars, who often commit far greater crimes than the Gypsies."

*   *   *   *

" The Gypsies in this country have for centuries been accused of child stealing ; and therefore it is not to be wondered at, that, when children have been missing, the Gypsies should be taxed with having stolen them.   About thirty years since, some parents who had lost a child, applied to a man at Portsmouth, well known in those days by the name of Payne or Pine, as an astrologer, wishing to know from him what was become of it.   He told them *to search the Gypsy tents for twenty miles round.*   The distressed parents employed constables, who made diligent search in every direction to that distance, but to no purpose ; the child was not to be found in their camps.   It was, however, soon afterwards discovered, drowned in one of its father's pits, who was a tanner.   Thus was this pretended astrologer exposed to the ridicule of those who, but a short time before, foolishly looked on him as an oracle.

" On another occasion the same accusation was brought against the Gypsies, and proved to be false.

---

* One Gypsy, I believe, has been convicted of having some stolen poultry in his tent ; but he had received it from the thief. No other fact of the sort has come to my knowledge.

The child of a widow at Portsmouth was lost, and after every search had been made on board the ships in the harbour, and at Spithead, and the pond. dragged in the neighbourhood, to no effect, it was concluded that the Gypsies had stolen him. The boy was found a few years afterwards, at Kingston-upon-Thames, apprenticed to a chimney-sweeper, He had been enticed away by a person who had given him sweetmeats; but *not by a Gypsy*."

* * * *

" The following anecdote will prove the frequent oppression of this people. Not many years since a collector of taxes in a country town said he had been robbed of fifty pounds by a Gypsy; and being soon afterwards at Blandford in Dorsetshire, he fixed on a female Gypsy as the person who robbed him in company with two others, and said she was in man's clothes at the time. They were taken up and kept in custody for some days: and had not a farmer voluntarily come forward, and proved they were many miles distant when the robbery was said to be perpetrated, they would have been tried for their lives, and probably hanged. The woman was the wife of William Stanley (who was in custody with her,) who now reads the Scriptures in the Gypsy tents near Southampton. Their wicked accuser was afterwards convicted of a crime for which he was condemned to die, when he confessed that he had not been robbed at the time referred to, but had himself spent the whole of the sum in question.

" Another Gypsy, of the name of Stanley, was

lately indicted at Winchester for house-breaking, and had not his friends at great expense proved an *alibi*, it is likely he might have been executed. And in this way have they been suspected and persecuted ever since the days of Henry the Eighth. They have been hunted ; their property has been taken from them ; themselves have been frequently imprisoned, and in many cases their lives taken ; or, which to many of them is much worse, they have been transported to another part of the world, for ever divided from their families and friends.

"In the days of Judge Hale, thirteen of these unhappy beings were hanged at Bury St. Edmonds, for no other cause than that they were Gypsies ; and at that time it was death without benefit of clergy for any one to live among them for a month. Lately, two of the most industrious of this people had a small pony and two donkeys taken away, merely on suspicion that they were stolen. They were apprehended and carried before a magistrate, to whom they proved that the animals were their own, and that they had legally obtained them. The cattle were then pounded for trespassing on the common, and if their oppressed owners had not had money to defray the expenses, one of the animals must have been sold for that purpose.

Not long ago, a Gypsy was suspected of having stolen lead from a gentleman's house. His cart was searched; but no lead being found in his possession, he was imprisoned for three months, for living under the hedges as a vagrant ; and his horse which was worth thirteen pounds, was sold to meet the demands of the constables. And another Gypsy, who had two horses in his possession, was suspected of having stolen them, but he proved that they were his property by purchase. He was committed for three months as a vagrant, and one of his horses was sold to defray the expenses of his apprehension, examination, &c.

"The author has just heard that a poor, aged, industrious woman, with whom he has long been acquainted, has had her donkey taken from her; and that a man with four witnesses swore that it was his property. The poor woman told a simple, artless tale to the magistrates, and was not fully committed. She was allowed two days to bring forward the person of whom she bought it. Conscious of her innocence, she was willing to risk a prison, if she could not recover her donkey and establish her character. After a great deal of trouble and expense in despatching messengers to bring forward her witnesses, she succeeded in obtaining them. They had no sooner made their appearance, than the accuser and his witnesses fled, and left the donkey to the right owner—the poor, accused, and injured woman.

"It cannot be expected that oppression will ever reform this people, or cure them of their wandering habits. Far more likely is it to confirm them in their vagrant propensities. And as their numbers do not decrease, oppression will only render them the dread of one part of their fellow-creatures, while it will make them the objects of scorn and obloquy to others."

*   *   *   *   *

" If they were driven to settle in towns, and could not, generally speaking, obtain employment, it might soon become necessary to remove all their children to their own parishes ; a measure not only very unhappy in itself, but one to which the Gypsies would never submit. Sooner would they die than suffer their children to go to the parish workhouse, at a distance from them."

*　　*　　*　　*　　*

" In this neighbourhood there was lately a sweeping of the commons and lanes of the Gypsy families. Their horses and donkeys were driven off, and the sum of £3 5s. levied on them as a fine, to pay the constables for thus afflicting them. In one tent, during this distressing affair, there was found an unburied child, that had been scalded to death, its parents not having money to defray the expenses of its interment. The constables declared to the author that it would make any heart ache to see the anguish the poor people were in when thus inhumanly driven from their resting places ; but, said they, *We were obliged to do our duty.* To the credit of these men, thirteen in number, it should be mentioned, that, with only one exception, they returned the fines to the people ; and one of them, who is a carpenter, offered a coffin for the unburied child, should the parish be unwilling to bury it.

" In this instance of their affliction and grief, the propensity to accuse these poor creatures was strongly marked, by a report charging them with having dug a grave on the common in which to bury it ; a circumstance very far from their feelings and general habits. The fact was, some person had been digging holes in search of gravel, and these poor creatures pitched their tent just by one of them.

"It was supposed by many in this neighbourhood, that the poor wretches thus driven away were gone out of the country; *but this was not the case.* They had only retired to more lonely places in smaller parties, and were all seen again a few days after at *a neighbouring fair.* This circumstance is sufficient to prove that they are not to be reclaimed by prosecutions and fines. It is therefore high time the people of England should adopt more merciful measures towards them in endeavouring to bring them into a more civilized state. The money spent in sustaining prosecutions against them, if properly applied, would accomplish this great and benevolent work. And without flattering any of its members, the author thinks the Committee at Southampton have discovered plans, wholly different from those usually adopted, which may prove much more effectual in accomplishing their reformation; for by these plans being put into prudent operation, many have already ceased to make the lanes and commons their home; and their minds are becoming enlightened, and their characters religious.

"In concluding this chapter, it may not be improper to remark, that, bad as may be the character of any of our fellow-creatures, it is very lamentable that they should suffer for crimes of which individually they are not guilty. Let us hope that, in reference to this people, unjust executions have ceased ; that people will be careful in giving evidence which involves the rights, liberties, and lives of their fellow-creatures, though belonging to the unhappy tribe of Gypsies ; and above all, let us hope that such measures will be pursued by the good and benevolent of this highly favoured land, as will place them in situations where they will learn to *fear God and honour the King*, and support themselves honestly in the sight of all men."

        *   *   *   . *   *

"In March, 1827, during the Lent Assizes, the author was in Winchester, and wishing to speak with the sheriff's chaplain, he went to the court for that purpose.   He happened to enter just as the judge was passing sentence of death on two unhappy men.   To one he held out the hope of mercy ; but to the other, *a poor Gipsy*, who was convicted of horse-stealing, he said, *no hope could be given.*   The young man, for he was but a youth, immediately fell on his knees, and with uplifted hands and eyes, apparently unconscious of any persons being present but the judge and himself, addressed him as follows : ' *Oh ! my Lord, save my life !*'   The judge replied, ' *No ; you can have no mercy in this world : I and my brother judges have come to the determination to execute horse-stealers ;* ESPECIALLY GYPSIES, *because of the increase of the crime.*'   The suppliant, still on his knees, entreated—'*Do, my Lord Judge, save my life ! do, for God's sake, for my wife's sake, for my baby's sake !*'   ' *No*,' replied the judge. ' *I cannot: you should have thought of your wife and children before.'* He then ordered him to be taken away, and the poor fellow was *dragged* from his earthly judge while on his knees. It is hoped, as a penitent sinner, he obtained the more needful mercy of God, through the abounding grace of Christ. After this scene, the author could not remain in court. As he returned, he found the mournful intelligence had been communicated to some Gypsies who had been waiting without, anxious to learn the fate of their companion. They seemed distracted.

" On the outside of the court, seated on the ground, appeared an old woman, and a very young one, and with them two children, the elder three years, and the other an infant but fourteen days old. The former sat by its mother's side, alike unconscious of her bitter agonies, and of her father's despair. The old woman held the infant tenderly in her arms, and endeavoured to comfort its weeping mother, soon to be a widow under circumstances the most melancholy. *My dear, don't cry,* said she, *remember you have this dear little baby.*"

* * * * *

" He could not forget the poor young widow whom he had seen in such deep distress at Winchester, and was led to resolve, if he should meet her again, to offer to provide for her children.

" Some weeks elapsed before he could hear any thing of her, till one day he saw the old woman sitting on the ground at the entrance of Southampton, with the widow's infant on her knee. ' Where

is your daughter?' he inquired. 'Sir,' she replied, 'she is my niece ; she is gone into the town.'
'Will you desire her to call at my house?' 'I
will, Sir,' said the poor old woman, to whom the
author gave his address.

"In about an hour after this conversation, the
widow and her aunt appeared. After inviting them
to sit down, he addressed the young woman thus :
—'My good woman, you are now a poor widow,
and I wished to see you, to tell you that I would
be your friend. I will take your children, if you
will let me have them, and be a father to them,
and educate them ; and, when old enough to work,
will have them taught some honest trade.' 'Thank
you, Sir,' said she ; 'but I don't like to part with
my children. The chaplain at the prison offered
to take my oldest, and send her to London to be
taken care of ; but I could not often see her there ;
I replied "I commend you for not parting with
her unless you could occasionally see her ; for
I suppose you love your children dearly.' 'Oh!
yes, Sir,' said the widow. The old aunt also added,
'*Our people set great store by their children.*"

*   *   *   *   *

"To those persons who are afraid of visiting the
Gypsies, lest they should be insulted, abused, and
robbed, the author may be allowed to say that they
have not the least grounds for such fears. In Scotland this fear is quite as general among the religious people as it is in England ; and in that country
the inhabitants are even afraid to prosecute them
for their depredations and crimes. In England,

ladies are frequently known to visit their camps singly, when more than a mile from towns, and to sit and read and converse with them for a considerable time, with the greatest confidence and safety.

"There is not the least prospect of doing them good by forcing instruction upon them. About the year 1748, the Empress Theresa attempted the improvement of the Gypsies in Germany, by taking away, by force, all their children of a certain age, in order to educate and protect them ; but such an unnatural and arbitrary mode of benevolence defeated its own object : and this is not to be wondered at : the souls of the free resist every effort of compulsion, whether the object be good or bad. Compulsory instruction, therefore, would do no good among the Gypsies. But they are easily won by kindness, and whoever wishes really to benefit them, must convince them that this is his intention by patiently bearing with the unpleasing parts of their characters, and by a willingness to lessen their distresses so far as it is in his power. Such kindness will never be lost upon them. Nor would the author recommend their *being encouraged to live in towns, except they were truly desirous of leading a new life, as it is almost certain that their morals would be greatly corrupted thereby : and they would be capable of more extensive injury to society, should they take to their wandering habits again.*"

  *   *   *   *

"A gentleman resident in one of the towns of Hampshire, was agreeably surprised one Sabbath morning by seeing a number of Gypsies at public worship ; and on being induced to converse with them, was pleased to find that they regularly attended divine service at Southampton, and other places. He directed them to move their tents into a more commodious situation in one of *his own fields.* This unusual act of kindness, which, however, required no great sacrifice on his part, made so deep an impression on the hearts of this people, as is not likely to be forgotten : they will speak of his kindness as long as they live.

"A lady once said to one of my friends, speaking of the Gypsies, ' My neighbours are always complaining that the Gypsies did them mischief, and rob them ; as for me, I cannot complain ; *I treat them kindly*, and in return, when they are near my house, they guard it, and frighten away other thieves. *I never lost any thing by having them near my house.*'

" The author has had similar testimonies from farmers, gentlemen and ladies of Sussex, Surrey, Hants, and Dorset, which prove that Gypsies can be honest and grateful."

* * * * *

" A king of England, of happy memory, who loved his people and his God better than kings in general are wont to do, occasionly took the exercise of hunting. Being out one day for this purpose, the chase lay through the shrubs of the forest. The stag had been hard run, and to escape the dogs had crossed the river in a deep part. As the dogs could not be brought to follow, it became necessary,

in order to come up with it, to make a circuitous
route along the banks of the river, through some
thick and troublesome underwood. The roughness
of the ground, the long grass and frequent thickets,
obliged the sportsmen to separate from each other;
each one endeavouring to make the best and speedi-
est route he could. Before they had reached the
end of the forest, the king's horse manifested signs
of fatigue and uneasiness; so much so, that his
Majesty resolved upon yielding the pleasures of the
chase to those of compassion for his horse. With
this view he turned down the first avenue in the
forest, and determined on riding gently to the oaks,
there to wait for some of his attendants. The
King had only proceeded a few yards, when, instead
of the cry of the hounds, he fancied he heard the
cry of human distress. As he rode forward, he
heard it more distinctly. 'Oh, my mother! my
mother! God pity and bless my poor mother!'
The curiosity and kindness of the sovereign led him
instantly to the spot. It was a little green plot on
one side of the forest, where was spread on the
grass, under a branching oak, a little pallet, half
covered with a kind of tent; and a basket or two,
with some packs, lay on the ground at a few paces
distant from the tent. Near to the root of the tree he
observed a little swarthy girl, about eight years of
age, on her knees, praying, while her little black
eyes ran down with tears. Distress of any kind
was always relieved by his Majesty, for he had a
heart which melted at 'human woe;' nor was it
unaffected on this occasion. And now he inquired

'What, my child, is the cause of your weeping?
For what do you pray?' The little creature at
first started, then rose from her knees, and pointing
to the tent, said, 'Oh, Sir! my dying mother!'
'What?' said his Majesty, dismounting and fast-
ening his horse up to the branches of the oak.
'What, my child? tell me all about it.' The
little creature now led the king to the tent;
there lay, partly covered, a middle-aged female
Gypsy, in the last stages of a decline, and in the
last moments of life. She turned her dying eyes
expressively to the royal visitor, then looked up to
heaven, but not a word did she utter; the organs of
speech had ceased their office; *the silver cord was
loosed, and the wheel broke at the cistern.* The
little girl then wept aloud, and stooping down,
wiped the dying sweat from her mother's face. The
King, much affected, asked the child her name,
and of her family, and how long her mother had
been ill. Just at that moment another Gypsy girl,
much older, came out of breath to the spot. She
had been at the town of W——, and had brought
some medicine for her dying mother. Observing
a stranger, she modestly curtised, and hastening to
her mother, knelt down by her side, kissed her
pallid lips, and burst into tears. 'What, my dear
child,' said his Majesty, 'can be done for you?'
'Oh, Sir!' she replied, 'my dying mother wanted
a religious person to teach her, and to pray with
her, before she died. I ran all the way before it
was light this morning to W——, and asked for a
minister, *but no one could I get to come with me to*

pray with my dear mother!' The dying woman seemed sensible of what her daughter was saying, and her countenance was much agitated. The air was again rent with the cries of the distressed daughters. The King, full of kindness, instantly endeavoured to comfort them : he said, '*I* am a minister, and God has sent *me* to instruct and comfort your mother.' He then sat down on a pack, by the side of the pallet, and taking the hand of the dying Gypsy, discoursed on the demerit of sin, and the nature of redemption. He then pointed her to Christ, the all-sufficient Saviour. While doing this, the poor creature seemed to gather consolation and hope ; her eyes sparkled with brightness, and her countenance became animated. She looked up—she smiled ; but it was the last smile ; it was the glimmering of expiring nature. As the expression of peace, however, remained strong in her countenance, it was not till some little time had elapsed, that they perceived the struggling spirit had left mortality.

" It was at this moment that some of his Majesty's attendants, who had missed him at the chase, and who had been riding through the forest in search of him, rode up, and found him comforting the afflicted Gypsies. It was an affecting sight, and worthy of everlasting record in the annals of kings.

" He now rose up, put some gold into the hands of the afflicted girls, promised them his protection, and bade them look to heaven. He then wiped the tears from his eyes, and mounted his horse.

His attendants, greatly affected, stood in silent admiration. Lord L——— was going to speak, but his Majesty turning to the Gypsies, and pointing to the breathless corpse, and to the weeping girls, said with strong emotion, ' Who, my lord, who thinkest thou, was neighbour unto these ? ' "

THE JEWS;

THEIR DISPERSION AND RESTORATION.

" Wanderers, rejoice ; the midnight gloom,
    Which holds your feet in error's maze,
And all the shadows of the tomb,
    Shall flee, dispersed by Gospel rays.

" Ye wayward flock, the time draws near,—
    The day by Israel's seers foretold,—
When Israel's Shepherd shall appear,
    Again to lead you to your fold.

" Yon orient beam, which streaks the dawn,
    Gives omen of the rising sun ;
Already see.the night withdrawn,—
    Already see the day begun."

THE history of the Egyptians has been so intimately connected with that of the Jews from remote antiquity, that a Treatise on the state and manners of the former, almost necessarily leads to a consideration of the present condition of the latter. There are, however, other reasons which induce me at this time to enter upon the subject. Attempts have been made for some years back, in several countries of Europe to bring the Jews more

H

prominently into public notice, for the ostensible
purpose of serving them, than was ever done before.   In this country, in particular, a Society has
for many years been formed for the express purpose of promoting their conversion to Christianity.
Jews and Gentiles are, I· believe, generally agreed,
that the time will come when the former shall be
gathered from all the countries in which they have
been, for so many centuries, scattered, to the land
of Judea, and, either in a temporal or spiritual
sense, or both, become a powerful nation, under
the immediate government of a Divine Ruler and
Lawgiver.

The Jews, under all circumstances, afford one of
the sublimest subjects, for the serious and attentive
consideration of Christians, that the history of the
world furnishes.   Their annals must silence, one
would think, the most obstinate caviller against the
evidence of prophesies and miracles.

Degraded as the Jews have been, in every sense
of the word, during seventeen hund red years, they
present at this day, as they have throughout the
whole of that long period, a spectacle more awfully
imposing and striking, than any other human beings ever did, or probably ever will do.

If animated nature constitute a more interesting
subject of contemplation, than the inanimate does,
then, of all animated nature, *man* affords that which
is of all others the most so ; and of all men the
Jews stand in that respect the first.

With what intense interest do we view, or even
read of a *city*, which, after having lain hid during

seventeen hundred years, has lately been discovered
in nearly the same state in which it then stood?
But what is this compared to what would have
been the case, could we have seen the *people themselves*, as they then were, in the same dress, with
the same peculiarities in their appearance; speaking the same language, having the same laws, observing the same customs, and the same ceremonies;
their civil and religious observances the same, and,
in short, being in every respect the very people
that they then were? This must have been, in an
incalculable degree, more interesting than merely
viewing their houses, their theatres, their tombs,
and their temples. Such a spectacle as this does
the Jewish People now afford to us! Nay, a much
more imposing one, inasmuch as they shew us a
people as they existed at a much more remote period. Probably they are little, if at all altered,
from the time when they were led away captive
out of the land of Judea, by Nebuchadnezzar to
Babylon: possibly they are in no great degree
changed, since their first obtaining possessions
of that long promised, and, now, long lost land,
to which, it is probable, they will in time be
restored.

We see then, in the Jews, a people who existed,
and as they existed, more than three thousand years
ago. This is not all, the Jews not only afforded us
a specimen of a people thus ancient, but also of a
people, in many respects, the most remarkable of
any that ever existed on the face of the earth; of
the chosen people of God: of a people whose king

was the Lord Jehovah, not in a figurative sense only, but as condescending to be *visibly* present with them, being their lawgiver, their instructor, and their defender. They consequently became, as it were, not only the depositories of God's word and will, but the organs through which He was pleased to make himself known to all the rest of the world. Hence, whatever little of light and truth is found mingled with the fables, the ceremonies, the worship, and traditions of benighted heathens, has been derived at one time or other by some means or other from this extraordinary people. This knowledge is often so greatly obscured and altered, as to be at first scarcely perceptible; but still it *may* be traced with a degree of certainty not to be mistaken.

Jesus Christ was born after the flesh, of a Jew. To them was the offer of salvation first made. They are the true olive-tree, whose root will never die, and whose branches will eventually cover the whole earth. They form the stock on which (its own branches being broken off) we have been grafted. But let us not boast as if we, the branches of the wild olive-tree, were nobler than the branches of the true olive-tree, because they have been broken off to make room for us! No; it was not for our superior excellence, but because of the unfruitfulness of the natural branches, that we have been engrafted in their stead. Let us, then, not be too high-minded, but fear. Let us stand by faith, for it was because of unbelief that they were broken off. But, though blindness is thus come upon Israel, it is but in part, and for a time. It is but till the *fulness of the Gentiles* shall be come in ; for then *all Israel* shall be saved. A Deliverer shall come out of Sion, and turn away ungodliness from Jacob. As we, in times past, when we believed not God received mercy through their unbelief ; so shall they (though not believing) eventually receive mercy through the mercy which we ourselves have received.

The whole of the prophesy above alluded to, (as contained in the 11th chapter of Romans,) is a most extraordinary, explicit, and full relation of events, past, passing, and approaching, relative to the Jews and Gentiles. The fulfilment of that wonderful part which has already occurred, and the equally wonderful part now fulfilling, are sure pledges, (if such could in a case like this be required,) that the remainder of the prophesy will, in the fulness of time, be accomplished with equal clearness and accuracy.

With the Jews, then, we Gentiles are, as it were, become one people. We are indirectly under the highest obligations to them ; we are the gainers, they are the temporary sufferers. On their stock we are growing and flourishing ; but they will be re-engrafted with us, and we shall eventually form together one tree, bearing the same fruit, under the care and culture of the same good Husbandman. This is, indeed wonderful ! This must, indeed, be the Lord's doing !

Let us not then boast against the branches (though they be for the present despised,) as though the *root* were ours; on the contrary, let us be humble, and cherish the branches which have been broken off to make room for us, and are waiting to be engrafted with us; remembering, that it is by *their* root that *we* are supported, and that, eventually both they and we must grow together. The time when this will be the case may not be far distant; the Gentiles seem to be fast coming in, and ere long the mercy which they shall have received may extend itself to the blessing of the long despised and oppressed Jews.

How far it may be the design of God to employ human agency in the bringing about of this last and greatest transitory event, belongs not to man to divine, nor does it perhaps become him to inquire. Let him await with faith and patience; when he is wanted, he will be called. In the mean time, there is a line of duty clearly chalked out for him, along which he may walk with confidence and safety. It is the path of *love!* love to God, and love to man: if he love not the latter, he cannot love the former. By this, and by this only, can we prove our claim to be the disciples of Jesus Christ: by this, and by this only, (as far as human means are concerned,) it is probable the Jews will be led to the embracing of Christianity: by the want of this, they have hitherto been repulsed and withheld, if not from embracing it, at any rate from thinking well of it. They have experienced every thing at the hands of Christians but that love and kindness which ought ever to distinguish them.

The history of the Jews (as dispersed among the countries professing Christianity,) exhibits one of the most, nay, the *most* revolting pictures of horrid cruelties that is to be found in the annals of the world. Nothing less than the hands of *Him* who had decreed their continuance as a distinct people could possibly have maintained them such, in every nation, in spite of attempts to extirpate them all.

Though the Gypsies have few, if any, of those peculiarities which distinguish, and tend to preserve the Jews a distinct people; they have not withstood those excessive and almost constant persecutions which the Jews have done. The former shun society and disregard wealth. They neither provoke by their intrusion, nor tempt to oppression by their great possessions. They have, therefore, escaped with comparatively few trials. They are contented with poverty, and they flee from contention. The Jews, on the contrary, in every country dread obscurity and poverty. They flock to the most populous cities, to the most crowded marts. They covet and pursue wealth with the most earnest and ceaseless avidity. So insatiable is their love of it, that, generally speaking, they are restrained by no fears but those of personal safety and freedom; nay they will even put those to a degree of risk, in the pursuit of riches, in a way which almost appears like the effect of madness. Even in times, and in countries, where there was scarcely a possibility of their retaining their riches when they had obtained them; but where, on the contrary, those riches, when ac-

quired, were almost certain to be the cause of their
ruin, they have always been as eager in their pursuit of them, as if their wealth was sure to remain
with them and to promote their safety and happiness.

This insatiable propensity in the Jews, to accu-
mulate riches, has been converted at different times
by the rulers of almost all countries, into a safe and
efficacious means of draining their own Christian
subjects of a considerable portion of their wealth.
The Jews have been compared to sponges which
will fill themselves with moisture in almost any place
or climate ; and which may be deprived of it, even
by the most violent means, till they contain not
another drop, without injuring either their powers,
or propensities to fill themselves again.   With
equal propriety and truth, they may be compared
to leeches, which mercenary rulers suffer and encourage to fasten on their people, that they may
satiate themselves with their blood ; who may then
be taken by those rulers, and squeezed until they
have disgorged whatever they have sucked in.   No
matter that a few of them lose their lives in the
operation, there are always more to be had.   This
experiment has been practised times without number, upon the poor infatuated Jews.   Indeed, the
cruelties which have been exercised upon them, by
those who professed to be Christians, during fourteen hundred years, are too shocking to relate, and
almost too horrible to be believed.

Notwithstanding all this, the Jews have forsaken
no country where they have once gained admission

and acquired wealth; still they are found (sometimes in the greatest numbers) in those places where
their entire extirpation has been most frequently
and most earnestly attempted. No sacrifices have
stood in the way of their keeping their stations;
they have professedly offered up their religion itself
on the altar of Mammon, and have even suffered
their sons and their daughters to be torn from them,
and educated to be what were called Christians,
rather than forsake a profitable mart.

It is said by the Jews themselves, that they have
forsaken *idolatry*, and they are, on that account,
in some instances, ready to question the justice of
God, in still continuing their degradations and their
afflictions, not considering that covetousness is
idolatry of the very worst description, as is expressly declared in both the Old and New Testa-
ments. The object of their idolatrous worship is
changed, but the disposition of the heart still re-
maineth, and the sin is the same. Let them look
to this. Let them purge the temple that is *within*.
Let them cast out thence the GOLDEN CALF, which
they have there set up, and have worshipped with
more devotion than they have done the Lord their
God, who brought them out of the land of Egypt—
than they have done Him to whom they look to
bring them out of all the countries whither-soever
He hath driven them. It was the worship of the
Golden Calf which deprived them of the Law
written with the finger of God on earthly tables of
stone; it is the worship of the Golden Calf which
deprives them of the covenant of grace written by

the Holy Spirit of God on the fleshly tables of the heart. Whatever they may think of Christians or of Christianity, they must acknowledge that purity of heart, and freedom from the inordinate love of wealth, are essential to the obtaining and retaining the blessing of the God of their fathers.

No people that ever lived on the face of the earth have had greater proofs afforded than that the providence of God ordereth all things; and that without holiness no man shall see the Lord. It must, however, as before observed, be acknowledged with sorrow and shame, that of Christians, and of Christianity, as affecting themselves, they have hitherto had little cause to think well. The precepts and spirit of Christianity they must allow to be pure; but they have ever, it must be acknowledged, found the conduct of its professors, as relating to them, totally at variance with that love which is declared to be its essence.

For the errors and misconduct of the Jews let us not, as professing Christians, hold ourselves blameless. Neither in our conduct towards them, nor even towards each other, have we evinced that compliance with the precepts of Christianity which is necessary to shew to others our own conviction of its truth and worth. During fourteen hundred years, have the Jews lived in constant, daily communication with Christians, in almost every Christian country, yet during all that long period, they have not in any one of those countries been uniformly shewn that brotherly kindness which Christianity particularly enjoins to be shewn to the unfortunate and the stranger. I am afraid that if we consider the Jewish people as the wayfaring man who fell among thieves, who stripped him of his raiment and wounded him, *we* shall be found to be the latter, instead of being, as we ought to have been, the good Samaritan, who poured oil and wine into his wounds, and took care of him.

In making any attempts to convert the Jews to Christianity, it would be both wise, and absolutely necessary to shew them that in its effects, Christianity is better than the religion which they profess, and which we call upon them to forsake. It is indispensable to let them see, to make them feel, that Christianity partakes more of that universal love and charity which fit it to become the religion of the world. Above all things, let us avoid tempting the Jews, in the remotest degree, to the profession of Christianity, by taking advantage of their inordinate love of worldly gain. While this desire keeps possession of the heart, the knowledge and love of Jesus Christ cannot find a place in it. I am afraid that in all the attempts to convert the Jews hitherto made, something of this appeal to their sorbid habits has been in some degree resorted to. In embracing Christianity, they should rather be led to expect to be called upon for a relinquishment of worldly advantages, for the Christianity which has these for its object, can have nothing of *vital* Christianity appertaining to it.

I am far from wishing to discourage any judicious endeavours to convert the Jews to Christianity; but if those attempts proceed in any instance, or in

any degree to either coercion or sordid induce-
ments, I most decidedly disapprove of them : they
cannot be of God, and therefore they must come
to nought. I would not have even the Christian
Scriptures in their own ancient languages forced,
or even urged upon them. Nay, I would not have
them even given without a full assurance being obtained, that the intentions of the receivers of them
was pure. Let us shew them the nature of true
Christianity, compelling us to love them and to
wish to serve them, and they may become by degrees desirous of examining the foundation of a religion which produces effects so advantageous to its
professors, to themselves, and to all mankind. Let
the loan of a Bible for a certain time be denied to
no one of them ; nor, on that Bible being returned,
with evidence of the borrower's having become acquainted with its contents, let the *gift* of it, if desired, be withheld. Beyond this, and if found
practicable, preaching to them and expounding the
nature of Christianity, I know not that at present
the attempt to convert them ought to be carried.
At any rate, I think that we should abstain from
seeking for, and taking, by any means, the children
of living Jews to educate as Christians. Our so
doing must cause considerable suspicion and jealousy among the conscientious Jews, and the parents
of such children—themselves continuing Jews—
cannot be actuated in so giving up their offspring
by any proper motives.

I am most decidedly of opinion, as before stated
that the best, perhaps the *only*, way in which we

can promote the conversion of the Jews, is by the purer practice in ourselves of Christianity. If the fulness of the Gentiles (whatever that may mean) must first come in, the promotion of that preceding event ought to be our primary object. I do not conceive that human agency will be excluded from the work of the restoration of the Jews, but I am inclined to believe that it will, at the same time, be accompanied with such an extraordinary display of the Divine presence and power, as will at once astonish and convince. Human agency is seldom, if ever, excluded from any of the great events of this world. Man, however, in such cases, is clearly only the instrument. The event is ordained, and man, unconsciously, perhaps unwillingly, aids in bringing it to pass.

The Jews were ordained by God, to be an unbroken chain, extending almost from the first peopling of the postdeluvian world, to its final destruction. Man has been endeavouring, throughout almost four thousand years, to break that chain; but what have those efforts served to prove?—his own weakness and blindness, and the power and foresight of God. Conqnered and enslaved; oppressed and massacred, the Jews have been, times almost innumerable, and in a degree never experienced by any other people; but what hath been the result? not that they have been extirpated, but that their conquerors, enslavers, and oppressors, have been hurled from their seats of power and grandeur—themselves and their palaces, their gods and their temples, have been swept away from the face of the earth : or if any memorials remain of them, they are such as only serve to exhibit to succeeding ages the folly, the weakness, and the mutability of all terrestrial things, which rest not on God's word or will, as a foundation.

Of all the mighty nations of antiquity which were opposed to the Jews, and by which they were oppressed, scarcely one remains, while they who were so repeatedly overcome and driven from their own country, still continue a numerous and united though dispersed people. The chain still remains unbroken, and there is strong evidence, both divine and human, to convince us that it will so remain to the final consummation of all terrestrial things.

The sceptic may say, that the ceremonious observances of the Jewish people are such, as of themselves to keep them a distinct people. Admit this, but they would have been insufficient to preserve them a people at all, throughout such persecution as must, in the usual course of events, have extirpated them long ago, in most, if not in all of the kingdoms and countries in which they have sought refuge. Their peculiar religious observances have, on the contrary, a strong tendency to produce, and increase, that persecution.

If God wills the preservation of a dispersed people, He wants not the assistance of peculiar religious observances in them, to aid Him in accomplishing his purposes. In fact, except circumcision and their Sabbath, scarcely any thing of their ceremonial law remains. The temple, the ark, priesthood and sa-

crifices, are taken from them. As to circumcision
and the Sabbath, the Mahomedans in all countries
have them.

Whatever the origin of the Gypsies may be ;
they are a people who, throughout many hundred
years at least, have been preserved a distinct
people, though more fully dispersed than even the
Jews themselves. No one, however can say, that
they have been preserved a distinct people by *their*
peculiar religious observances, *for they have none.*
This, then, *must* be God's doing !

THE JEWS;

AS CONNECTED WITH THE GYPSIES.

" The lost, the weary, and the wanderer :
O, these were once the objects of the Saviour's love.
Had He a heart that melted with compassion ?
It was for them.   Had He a tear to shed,
A blessing to bestow ?—It was for them.
Had He a word of peace, of righteousness,
Of comfort and advice ?—It was for them.
Had He a cross to bear, a death to die,
A sacrifice to make with his own blood ?
It was for them.   Had He a crown to win,
A rest to purchase, mansion to prepare,
A paradise to gain ?—It was for them ;
The lost, the weary, and the wanderer."

How wonderfully would it add to the grandeur and
impressiveness of the Jewish preservation, if it
should prove, as I have surmised, that the Gypsies
are the Egyptians, contemporaneous with the Jews
from the beginning ?   That, like the Jews, they
were doomed for their sins to the vilest degradation
and the most severe sufferings, a dispersed, but distinct people, in almost every nation under heaven :
—That after a certain period they, too, should be
again gathered to their own country, as pioneers,
or leaders of the way, to the Jews, to whose sins

and dispersion they had so greatly conduced! If
all this should prove to be the case, how greatly
will it add to the sublimity of the Jewish restoration! A secondary chain, from its formation, run-
ning parallel to, but totally distinct from the other,
through four thousand years, and at last uniting
with it, never again to be separated!

The sins of the people of God have been from
the first so intimately connected with, and owing
to the idolatrous Egyptians, that it can scarcely be
wondered at that God should condemn them together, that their punishment should be nearly similar, or that their recal and forgiveness should be
nearly at the same time. No sooner had God
chosen Abraham to be the father of his favoured
people, and had declared his purpose to him, and
given him his especial blessing, than his connexion
with the Egyptians, and his distrust of the Lord his
God began together. There was a famine in the
land of Canaan (his promised inheritance,) when,
instead of trusting in the aid of his Almighty Protector, who had so recently evinced his peculiar
favour towards him, his faith failed him, and he fled
to the worshippers of idols for support. As one
error generally leads to another, so it was with
Abraham, as he could not trust the Lord to feed
him, neither dared he to confide in Him for protection : but trusted rather to subterfuge, deception,
and a fiction to do it.

The connexion between the Egyptians and the
Israelites, thus begun in weakness and in fraud,
continued, as might be expected, ever afterwards

(with a slight temporary exception,) in injustice, cruelty, oppression, contention, deception, and hatred. They both of them grievously offended the Righteous Governor of the Universe; and, therefore, He appears to have judged it right to preserve them both distinct people, and to disperse them through every nation *(the one people in the cities, and the other in the fields and desolate places)* as constantly living evidences of *his* power and justice in both situations. That there might not exist any room to attribute these wonderful events to the effect of chance, He enabled and commanded his prophets to proclaim, ages before they occurred, both to them and to all people, that such was the determination of Divine wisdom.

Whatever hath been here said on the subject of the Jews must, I think, be admitted to be founded on the ground and evidence of Scripture, and of the experience of all civilized nations during many hundred years. Much of what has been advanced respecting the Gypsies may be considered by many as in some degree fanciful. Still it must be admitted by all, that they are a most extraordinary people, and that their origin and destination, as well as all their peculiarities, are deserving of the most serious consideration of all classes of reflecting men, and unaccountable on any other supposition than that of a miraculous interference.

Nothing that has been heretofore surmised on the subject appears at all satisfactory or convincing. That which has been here adduced may not appear to some perons to be much more so; but may at any rate afford a clue which may lead more profound and persevering examiners into the road of truth.   I cannot, however, perceive that the supposition, as far as it goes, is inconsistent with either the scriptural history of the Egyptians, with God's power and justice, or with the circumstances in which the Gypsies were first found, and in which they have continued ever since.   Those circumstances are so peculiar, and so opposed to what is called the natural course of events, that it appears to me that nothing short of a decree of the Almighty, ordaining their continuance under them, can possibly serve to account for their so doing. In fact, the two occurrences of the dispersion of the Jews, with their subsequent recal and exaltation, and that of the Egyptians, are so similar in their nature, their cause and their results,— they are so alike in the evidence to support them and in the prophesies which predicted them, that they must, it seems to me, stand or fall together. The same prophets, often at the same time—with equal force and clearness—foretell the future destiny of each.   Those predictions, as far as they have yet gone, are as fully accomplished in the one instance as in the other ; and if in the result, the Egyptians are not restored to their own country, becoming a kingdom, though (as perhaps compared with that of the Jews) a base kingdom and under a Saviour and a Great One, learning to know the Lord, then will the word of prophesy fail as completely as if the Jews themselves were never to be recalled.

It may be said, we know where the Jews are, and that there is still such a people in existence ready to be recalled, but where are the Egyptians? Supposing no such people were known to exist, still they must appear from some quarter, or the prophesies must fail; nay, they must fail if those long lost Egyptians were not found exactly in the state that those extraordinary people the Gypsies are now in — a state which of itself proclaims a miraculous origin and support—a state that, on any other supposition, is a complete paradox, yet a state that in every feature, extraordinary as they all are, resembles the predicted state of the Egyptians during their dispersion :—people coming, no one could tell where from, no one could tell whence, dispersed almost at once over most of the then known kingdoms of the earth, without a home, cast into the *open fields*, never leaving them, despised even by the most despicable; without a God, without idols, without images; with complexions, and, as far as is known, every thing resembling the long lost ancient Egyptians!   Do we then need to ask where are the Egyptians to be found?   Are they not in all lands? Are they not in the open fields of this and of almost all the kingdoms of the earth, whither the Lord God hath cast them out, as his prophets predicted, and from whence He will, when the fulness of time shall come, recal them, and in fulfilment of the same predictions, replace them, in their native land, teaching them with all mankind, to know and to serve *Him* who constituted them no unimportant link in the long unbroken chain of a wise and merciful Providence? The wonder then will not be that such a people should have been at length discovered, but that, possessing as we have always done, such clear prophesies respecting the ancient Egyptians, and possessing likewise a people so manifestly resembling them, that we should never before have discovered even the similitude, especially when the extraordinary state of the Gypsies itself was such as to demand the most strict attention.

I think that we must not only admit the ancient Egyptians to be some where a dispersed people in the open fields of all countries, whither the Lord God, as predicted, hath driven them; but also, that the Gypsies are that people so dispersed, and that they, as well as the Jews, probably nearly at the same time, will each be recalled and reassembled in their respective countries; both of them there to be brought, through the instrumentality of a Saviour, to that knowledge of the Lord, which is displayed in the Christian Scriptures. These two extraordinary people seem then, as designed, to connect the commencement of the postdiluvian world with its termination; constituting, throughout its whole course, perpetual miracles to the confounding of every sceptic who shall dare to deny the existence of such miraculous interference of the Almighty in the government of the universe, and of its inhabitants: for, however, they might ascribe the existence of such people, under such circumstances, to natural causes, yet they must admit them to be circumstances such as could not possibly be guessed to be likely to happen before they took place. Now, then, as no one of these sceptics can deny that such incredible, if not impossible, events were clearly foretold by men professing to be prophets, ages before they occurred, they must, one would think, admit an imparted foreknowledge of future events. But it is not with sceptics that I mean to have to do, if I can convince believers in God and in Christ, that I am right in my surmisings, I shall be satisfied; nay, if I can rouse them to such a research as shall finally lead to the discovery and establishment of the *truth*, I shall not only be satisfied but thankful. The investigation at any rate can neither be misplaced, uninteresting, nor unimproving.

CONCLUSION.

***

" The Lord is not slack concerning his promise, as some
    men count slackness :—for one day is with the Lord
    as a thousand years, and a thousand years as one
    day.—2 Peter, iii. 8 and 9.

***

Circumstances have for a long time been conduc-
ing to draw the attention of the world, the Christian
world in particular, to the subject here treated of.
A strong conviction is becoming very prevalent,
that the long predicted events relating to the Jews,
are fast, and nearly approaching ; whether, then,
that prediction be well or ill founded, a supposition,
such as I have brought forward respecting the
Gypsies, cannot, I think, be treated with indiffer-
ence. This inquiry seems, indeed, naturally to
lead to the investigation of many other parts of
God's government of the world, even from the
creation itself, to which, in its commencement,
it so nearly approximates. More particularly it leads
to the contemplation of man in his subsequent advancement even from the first steps in civilization,
knowledge, and holiness.

The information, which it hath pleased Almighty
God to afford us of man and occurrences in para-

dise, or even before the flood, are scanty and brief indeed. We are therefore bound to believe, that more was unnecessary. A single page contains the first, and a very few more, the whole of the latter, though comprising the history of the world during two thousand years. That men were born, had certain names given them, lived, had children, and died, comprises almost the whole of the records respecting that first period in the existence of our fallen race.

What might have been the condition of the inhabitants of paradise, had man continued in a state of innocence, obedient to the commands of his Creator, we know but little. Whether the paradisaical test of his obedience, as related to us, be literally described, or only figuratively, is but of perhaps little importance ; one thing, however, is clear, man was a being possessed of free-will ; capable of choosing the good and rejecting the evil. It is likewise clear, that happiness was the reward of obedience, and that he lost it because he transgressed the command. The duty required, like all which God enjoins, was in its nature a blessing, and so easy that it could in its performance merit nothing: the gift, then, though conditional, was clearly of grace ; but being given, the reward for obedience was as certain, as it would have been had the task enjoined been infinitely more important than it was. It is likewise clear, that had man continued obedient, he would not have been subject to death, but would have enjoyed everlasting happiness. But having by disobedience forfeited this blissful inheritance, God seems to have decreed a total and dreadful change in his state on earth. Debased in his nature, and doomed to more or less of inevitable sin and misery during life, he was to suffer the penalty of his offences here by a painful removal from this state of existence. It, however, appears to have been the will of the Almighty, with whom one day is as a thousand years, and a thousand years as one day, gradually to elevate man on earth till he should—when the fulness of time was come,—be enabled to attain eternal felicity, at least equal to that which might have been enjoyed by him, had he remained obedient in paradise.

What man was, immediately subsequent to the fall, or even during the almost two thousand years preceding the deluge, we know little. That he was very inferior to what he is now, appears, however, very evident. Though most of the human inhabitants of this earth lived then from five hundred to almost a thousand years, and therefore must have increased in numbers very rapidly, the advancement that was made by them in arts, sciences, and general civilization, seems to bear no proportion to the advancement that they made in the same, in a fourth part of the period subsequent to the flood, when cities of vast extent, and almost inconceivable splendour and strength, were soon erected. The utmost that we learn of the works of the antidiluvians is, that Enoch built a city, and that Jabal, Tubal Cain, and Jubal, who were brethren (living fifteen hundred years after the fall,) were the *fathers* of such as dwell in tents, of such as have cattle,

of such who work in iron and brass, and of all
such as handle the harp and the organ (whatever
those instruments might then be.)   The progress
of the antidiluvians in wickedness seems to have
been the greatest advancement that they made.   In
fact, they appear to me to the last, to have proceeded scarcely beyond that line of civilization,
within which we should now include the lowest of
our species.

The first great step then, which, by God's appointment, occurred in man's advancement, was at
the deluge.   After that event, his intellectual progress seems to have been rapid and great.

A question here occurs, which is at least highly
curious, if not greatly important.   Were Noah
and his family *negroes?* or in what degree were
they removed from being so?   From them, we are
taught to believe, that all subsequent human beings
have sprung; all deviations then from them which
now exist, whatever they may be, must have taken
place since then.   As it clearly appears to have
been the plan of Divine Providence, gradually to
advance mankind both in external and internal
good qualities and acquirements; and as, within
modern times, many instances have occurred of
the native coloured inhabitants of various countries being extirpated, and replaced by whites, does
it not seem probable that the unenlightened inhabitants of the antidiluvian world were negroes;
and that finally that race of human beings will
cease to exist?

In corroboration of this supposition of the gradual advancement of mankind from Negroes of different degrees of what we now consider finer skins, features, and forms, I insert the following extract, from a work, entitled the "Costume of the Ancients"—by Thomas Hope, Vol. 2.—London, 1812; page 1. :—

"The ancient Egyptians were descended from the Ethiopians, and while their blood remained free from any mixture with that of European or Asiatic nations, their race seems to have retained obvious traces of the aboriginal negro form and features. Not only do the human figures in their coloured hieroglyphics display a deep swarthy complexion, but every Egyptian monument, whether statue or bas-relief, presents the splay feet, the spreading toes, the bow-bent shins, the high meagre calves, the long swinging arms, the sharp shoulders, the square flat hands, the head when seen profile, placed not vertically but obliquely on the spine, the jaws and chin consequently very prominent, together with the skinny lips, depressed nose, high cheek bones, large unhemmed ears, raised far above the level of the nostrils, and all the other peculiarities characteristic of the negro conformation. It is true the practice prevalent among the Egyptians of shaving their heads and beards close to the skin, (which they only deviated from when in mourning) seldom allows their statues to shew that most undeniable symptom of negro extraction, the woolly hair; the heads of their figures generally appearing covered with some sort of cap, or when bare, closely shaven. In the few Egyptian sculptured personages, however, in which the hair is introduced, it uniformly offers the woolly texture, and the short crisp curls of that of the negroes; nor do I know a single specimen of genuine Egyptian workmanship, in which are seen any indications of the long sleek hair, or loose wavy ringlets of Europeans or Asiatics."

A writer in the *British and Foreign Review* for April, 1836, on Egypt, says, " It may appear surprising, but, perhaps it would scarcely derogate from the physical beauty of the Egyptian people, male and female, if we ascribed to them the negro features; that is, the undegraded negro features, as represented on the monuments. They are black, and have woolly hair, it is true, but they are decidedly the finest men of all the varieties of the human species, which have been exhibited. They are superior in profile, in deportment, in attitude, and in figure. This is a consideration deserving the notice of the advocates of negro slavery. They are, in fact, not the negroes blasphemously supposed by them to have the mark of Cain inflicted on them; brutalized by long ages of misgovernment in their own country, and degraded by the branding iron and the lash of their European taskmasters in the West Indies; but negroes, such as late travellers have described in St. Domingo, where the chains of slavery have been a long time broken, and the negro child has drawn his first breath in freedom. They are the negroes such as they were originally formed, and as they come from the hands of their Maker. We now leave that consideration to physiognomists. The moral effects of slavery and degraded habits, or *vice versa*, in depressing or elevating the scale of physical beauty, is quite worthy of their attention.

" We have said that there are some exceptions to the general rule, that the Egyptian people were not distinguished by the negro character. Two of the exceptions are singularly in accordance with the foregoing remarks ; they relate to Memnon and his mother. It has often been discussed, and inferred from the circumstances of Memnon being called black by Virgil, corroborated by the designation employed by Herodotus respecting the Egyptians, of their being black, with crisped hair, that Memnon was a negro. That fact, as we have shown, would not preclude him from being the handsomest man next to Achilles, at the seige of Troy. But by a curious accident, proved by the illustrations of Rosellini and Champollion, it is now ascertained that Memnon was half a negro, his mother being an actual negress. His mother, wherever represented, is not only black, but always exhibits the purely negro character ; and Memnon himself, though only half a negro in blood, approaches the negro in his facial outline, as may be readily seen by a copy of the great statue on the plain of Thebes, now in the British Museum, more than any of the entire line of native Egyptian princes."

Great, however, as the step appears to have been which, at or immediately after the flood, man seems to have been enabled to take towards a state of greater perfection ; it was but a very trifling one to what had at the fall been promised, but which was reserved for subsequent generations, when the Son of God, taking our nature upon Him, was to bring life and immortality to light, himself leading the way, to be followed in it by those who should be found to be more immediately *his.* Till then man was kept in deep darkness of ignorance respecting a future state of existence.

Though very soon after the flood, God was pleased in a most especial manner to manifest his Divine presence, and afford his explicit directions for man's conduct through life, with a promise of rewards for obedience, and a denunciation of punishment for transgressions: those rewards and punishments were all of a temporal nature. The next step of man then was not, as *now,* to immortality. The directions of God, therefore, for his government were very different in their nature from those which *we,* as joint heirs with Christ of immortality, have received. The covenant which God made with them, was a temporary covenant of *blood;* that which He hath since been graciously pleased to make with *us,* is an everlasting covenant of *love.* We must not, therefore, be surprised that the permissions, and even commands given to them by the Almighty, under the preparatory law, were such as would be inconsistent with that purer spiritual law —never to be broken—which hath been given by Him (when the fulness of the time was come,) to us.

Thus far it hath appeared necessary to premise, in order to account for much of God's dealings with mankind previous to the advent of our Saviour's appearance upon earth. Man, however, is not even now elevated to the state of exaltation, and comparative perfection, for which, in the wise and merciful counsels of his God, he is declaredly destined.

He has indeed received at the hands of his Saviour, a religion that is pure and perfect. But he has corrupted it, till it now often scarcely retains a trace of its original simplicity and pure spiritual nature. His Saviour and Lawgiver hath already appeared in *humility* on earth, to set him an example of perfection that he might—if he would—follow his steps. Man, however, hath forsaken the path in which the Saviour strove to lead him. That despised and forsaken Saviour, we are, nevertheless, taught, will again appear on earth, but in *power* and in great *glory*. Then will man attain to his utmost state of earthly perfection and felicity. Then will the religion of Christ be stripped of all those encumbrances and defilements, with which mistaken zeal—vanity—folly, and worldly-mindedness, have disguised and corrupted it. Then will there remain nothing to keep sincere believers from worshipping God in union and brotherly love together. They will then be all of one mind, and of one spirit. It will then be no longer necessary to say—" know the Lord,"—for all will then know Him, and be taught of Him. Thus, then, it hath been attempted to be shewn, that it is the plan of Divine Providence gradually to advance (on the whole) man on earth in the scale of mortal existence, notwithstanding the many instances of partial deterioration, which may cause some to exclaim " Where is the promise of his coming?"

To return, however, to the earlier stages of man's existence on earth. So little advancement appears to have been made before the flood in any of the

arts and sciences, that it is probable that the ante-
diluvians were totally unacquainted with any kind
of writing.   Noah must have been ignorant of any
such art, or the method would have become general
among all his descendants in the rising nations of
the infant world.   This evidently was not the case,
for they eventually adopted different methods of so
conveying information to distant people.   How
early *alphabetical* writing was invented and practised, seems not discoverable, though it was probably
not very long after the flood.   Rocks and stones,
and iron pens, seem to have been the earliest rude
implements employed.   In this art, the Egyptians
appear to have been the most deficient, hieroglyphical
writing—that which they adopted, and in which
they persevered — being the most imperfect and
tedious method of all others.   This, however, it is
probable, was the first system practised.

In those primeval times it appears to have been
God's method, Himself to give more immediate direction than in these latter ones ; and it is far from
improbable that a nation, making such rapid progress in intellectual attainments as the Egyptians
did, had been favoured, in an especial manner, by
divine communications of the will of God ; but that
(like the Jews in latter times,) they forsook their
Divine King and Lawgiver, electing a *man* for their
king, and stocks and stones for their gods.   That
the former was the case, within less than four hundred years from the flood, is evident from the relation of the life of Abraham, who fled to Egypt for
preservation from famine, and was there noticed by

its *king*. Thus early began the connection between the Egyptians and the Jews, even in the life time of the great father and founder of the latter nation. This connection, it appears to me, has never once entirely ceased, during almost four thousand years, nor, probably, ever will cease to the end of time. That the Egyptians were the first, or among the first idolaters, seems very certain ; as well as that they were instrumental in leading the Israelites into the same abominable practice.

This early connection, thus begun in sin, has ever since served constantly to display to the rest of the world, the power, the faithfulness, the justice, the stedfastness, and finally, the mercy of Almighty God. All these have been displayed, and are still displaying in a manner too remakable to be over-looked, and too strong and clear to be misconceived, excepting by the most prejudiced or inattentive observer. These wonderful and according miracles have not only been exhibited by the people of both these nations in almost all the countries of the earth, but they have been exhibited in such a manner, as that none might plead ignorance of their existence, the one people having been driven by the arm of the Almighty into the *cities* of all lands, and the other, as predicted, into the *open fields* of the same. Yet that they might not again tempt each other to offend, though thus brought near together in all countries, they have in all been kept so separate, as to remain ignorant that they were the two people for ages united in working iniquity, each still remaining in that predicted mental darkness, inflicted

upon them till the time appointed for their en-
lightenment shall arrive.

Awful, tremendous, and appalling indeed, it
seems, are to be the circumstances by which the
final restoration of the Jews is to be ushered in.
It would seem as if all the nations of the earth were
to be cast into the fiery furnace of God's justice;
there to be all amalgamated into one mass, in order
that all impurities may be carried off by absorption,
or in base dross, till the residue be purer than fine
gold itself; for the elect's sake, however, it may be
that those days may not only be shortened, but
much of the dreadful inflictions remitted.

The state in which the Jews have remained during almost two thousand years, has been considered,
I believe, almost universally as miraculous, because
it is considered that, in what is called the natural
course of events, they must, in many instances at
least, have become incorporated with the people of
the countries in which they have, for hundreds of
years, resided. Admitting this in respect of the
Jews, how is it possible not to draw the same inference from the equally extraordinary state in which,
for many hundreds of years, another people (the
Gypsies) have remained dispersed throughout almost
every country in the world, and kept equally with the
Jews a distinct and separate people; rarely inter-
marrying with others, and never amalgamating, or
becoming incorporated with the inhabitants of any
countries in which they have so long resided.

We have seen that prophecies equally clear and
strong, by the same prophets, foretel the extra-

ordinary dispersion and continuance as a separate
people, of the Egyptians, as fully as they do those
of the Jews; both prophecies likewise foretelling
the final restoration to, and exaltation of, each of
these people in their own original countries.

Either, then, we must give up the assumed conclusion, that the state of the Jews proves a miraculous interference, preserving their continuance as a
distinct people, under their extraordinary circumstances, or we must admit the no less extraordinary
circumstances of the Gypsies to have an equal
claim to a miraculous foundation. Taken together,
they appear mutually to support and illucidate each
other; and it seems to me that they must stand
or fall together. The condition of the Jews as
foretold, and as it at this time exists, is a
stupendous display of Almighty power exhibited,
century after century, to all the nations of the
earth, in their towns and their cities. The condition of the Gypsies—as descendants of the ancient Egyptians—is an equally stupendous display
of the same Almighty power exhibited, century
after century, to almost all the same nations of the
earth, in their open fields. When, then, we contemplate these the two mightiest among the nations of the early post-diluvian world, intimately
connected from their commencement, both most
highly offending their Almighty Creator, and both
consequently drawing down upon their guilty heads
—thousands of years ago—the most extraordinary
denunciations that ever were uttered by the voice
of man in obedience to the commands of God,—the

stupendousness of the event becomes increased in a manifold degree. When, also, it is further considered, that these denunciations were to be thousands of years in fulfilling, and that the events predicted were of a nature such as the imagination of man could scarcely either have conceived or admitted ; and yet further, that they both did commence at the time foretold,—that century after century,—through more than two thousand years, —they have continued to proceed in their predicted and appointed course towards their final important consummation, the magnitude and astonishing nature of the miracle, seem even further increased. It is yet more so, when it is considered, that these extraordinary events, so far from being promoted, or willingly furthered by the people, or governments of the countries into which the strangers obtruded themselves, have almost invariably been opposed and attempted to be frustrated by them. Farther, this miracle appears still more astonishing, when it is considered, that these two extraordinary people have been so far from aiding each other in obtaining entrance into, and remaining in the respective countries in which they had taken refuge, that they are almost the only people who have never had any communication with each other. The one, as predicted, pertinaciously adhering in poverty to the *open fields* of every country in which they were scattered ; whilst the others, with equal pertinacity, sought refuge, and riches, in the most populous towns and cities, avoiding the open fields and a pastoral life as an abomination.

Thus are these two once mighty people,·who, in the earlier ages of the world, were continually transgressing together the commandments of their Almighty Creator, and uniting to substitute the workmanship of their own hands in the place of Him who made the heavens and the earth,—cast out and dispersed, throughout all the earth—without a temple, an idol, an image, forsaken of God,—obtruders, contemned, and persecuted, a bye-word and a reproach to the most despicable of mankind ; a dreadful and notable example of the vengeance of an offended God, spread throughout the cities and the fields of almost every land on the face of the earth, and doomed so to continue till such an impressive example shall be no longer neces-sary.

Of all the numerous other nations, contempora-ries with, and opposed to the Jews, which have since ceased to exist as nations, the people have in no one instance continued distinct to the later times. They have invariably been destroyed, lost among, or incorporated with their conquerors.   Nor were there any prophetic intimations that they should so continue.   The Jews and the Egyptians were the only two people whose perpetuation to after times was foretold, with the manner of each, and they two, and they two alone have so continued, and continued with those extraordinary peculiari-ties and wonderful circumstances attached to them, in which the prophets foretold that they should long remain.   All these unprecedented events hav-ing occurred exactly as predicted many ages be-

fore, afford strong presumptive evidence, if not assurance, that the remainder of the extraordinary
prophecies will, in due time, be equally fulfilled.
The time when, and the manner how, are not so
clearly foreshewn. Many reasons may be assigned,
and others probably exist unknown to us, why in
these respects man should be kept in ignorance
till the fulness of the time is come. Then all
mysteries may, and probably will be cleared up,
and the wisdom and mercy, as well as importance
of the predicted and then accomplished events,
will be manifested to the astonished and adoring
world.

The character of the Gypsies, as it has been here
described, appears to me to be so extraordinary for
a whole race of people so situated as they are,
" *scattered* among all nations, and dispersed in all
countries," that I think nothing but the fiat of the
Almighty, impressing it upon them for a particular
purpose, can possibly account for it. All their propensities, their habits, and their manners, are calculated for a people doomed to a continuance in
such a state, and for such a people only. While so
strong are those propensities, those habits, and those
manners, that no measures, however severe or violent, have yet been able either to eradicate or weaken
them. If the Gypsies could obtain a livelihood
without ever coming in contact with other people,
it seems as if they would rather do so. Nay, they
will submit to the greatest and most severe privations rather than be compelled to such an alterna-
tive. When they are driven to it, it seems that

their object is to retire from it again as soon as the means of so doing can be acquired. If, by the severity of the weather, or other causes, they are forced to seek refuge under less penetrable roofs than those of their frail, slight tents,—they never resort to the common lodging houses, among the depraved vagrants of towns ; they obtain a room to themselves, however mean it may be ; they dwell as retired and unknown as they can, and they leave their prison house, like the earliest sportive denizens of the air, on the first gleam of sunshine, to enjoy their beloved freedom in the refreshing breeze of the opening spring, erecting their own simple endeared habitation in the verdant lane, under the budding hawthorn, by the side of the sparkling stream, whose banks are sweetened and embellished by the violet and the primrose, while the heavens smile over their heads with renewed splendour, and the whole welkin rings with the awakened notes of love, and harmony, and delight. Oh ! can we hold beings like these in scorn and contempt ?

This unconquerable love of freedom, and of the country, is not felt, in the same degree, by any other people on the face of the globe, as it is felt by the Gypsies, universally, and has been so, through all the ages since they were first known. It seems inseparable from their nature, and must have been impressed upon it, for some good purpose by Almighty power. What that purpose is, I think no one can now doubt. There seems likewise to have been given to them a degree of intellectual power possessed by no other people at all in the same low

station ; with a freedom from cringing meanness, or
abject servility, which tends greatly to preserve them
a free and independent people.   Though they will
accept of alms, and even ask for them, it is, in general, only of such persons as happen to come in
their way.   They rarely, if ever, beg from door to
door, or in towns ; and never with whining or fic-
titious distress.   It is an extraordinary circumstance that, however distressed, they rarely apply
for that legal relief which they might demand.
There is an unaccountable quickness and clearness of understanding possessed by them, which not
only enables them to express themselves clearly,
but also to turn the failings of others to their own
account.   At the same time, their language is neither profane nor vulgar, but generally such as is
proper and approaching to refinement.   Though
they cannot be accused of false modesty, to those
who do not encourage ribaldry, their language is
seldom other than decent and unassuming.   On all
occasions they seem to avoid giving unnecessary
offence in conversation.   Since they have ceased to
be persecuted and hunted as wild beasts, or to be
considered as houseless thieves and vagabonds, few
instances of convictions of *real* Gypsies, have
been known.   To these qualities, contributing to
fit them for their assigned station in the "*open
fields* of all countries," may be added their unprecedented contentedness with the very scantiest, meanest, and even most revolting food.   Not,
as has been said, because they prefer it ; but, as
Boswell said, because they are often very ill off for

want of victuals of any kind, and must, therefore, put up with such as they can get. Their abstemiousness, and contentedness with little and mean food, is requisite for a people who are doomed, like them, to be cast into, and remain in, the " wilderness and the *open fields*." Such a people, one might suppose, would be an *idle* race. This is not the case, generally speaking ; they are industrious so far as they can be so consistently with their decreed stations in the world ; so that there are few trades, which it admits of, which they do not follow : they do not seek to eat the bread of idleness, but they will not drag the chains of slavery. If it were not for their industry, they could not appear so decently clad as they very generally do, nor with the comfortable accommodations which they often possess.

That God, who has thus decreed, for a time, the continuance of these people in this extraordinary state of separation from the rest of mankind, in all the countries throughout which *He* has " *scattered*" them,—has been mercifully pleased to add a peculiar blessing to their obedience, *the blessing of almost uninterrupted health.* They are rarely sick, generally live to a good old age ; sometimes to a very great one, and are then generally taken good care of. To medicines and medical men they are strangers. Healthy during life, they are generally removed from it without paying the tax which wealth imposes, that of procrastinated sufferings to themselves, and of anxious misery to their friends. They move from place to place, but not in *search* of

health, for they take it with them, while the sons
and daughters of affluence spend their time, and
their money, and often the money of others, in the
vain search after it.   The Gypsies, therefore, need
not forsake their assigned station to be near the
doctor.   Temperance, exercise, fresh air, and freedom from the cares attendant on acquiring, keeping, or spending wealth, are to them preservatives
better than the most efficacious remedies.   Their
women suffer but little from child-bearing, and
their children little from nursing.   When stationary the infants are left pretty much to take care of
themselves or one another ; and when on the tramp,
a bag on the mother's back serves both to hold
them and to preserve the free use of their limbs.   A
naturally deformed Gypsy is scarcely known.   Both
men and women are well shaped.   The young women, though often both elegantly formed and handsome, are rarely, if ever, found as common prostitutes in towns.   They generally marry young
among themselves.

The foregoing circumstances are all calculated
to keep the Gypsies attached to that station and
mode of living, which seems clearly to have been
assigned them.   To these, however, other peculiar
propensities or habits may be mentioned as contributing to the same effect.   They have no desire to
practise or obtain those arts, which embellish and
elevate man in society.   Though, if asked, they
would generally *say* that they should *like* to learn
to read ; yet I believe that they have rarely, if ever
been eager to do so, or to accept of an offer of being

taught, or even of having their children instructed. The fact is, that there appears evidently to be an innate avoidance of every thing that would seem to have a tendency to draw them into more intimate connexion with other people. Of this, perhaps, they themselves may not be fully aware : it, however, is so, and must be necessary to produce and to continue, for so long a period, an anomaly so striking in human nature. They never seem to make the least attempts to delineate any objects in any way. They know nothing of poetry ; though one would suppose, passing the life that they do, and possessing the strong sense and feelings which they certainly have, they would be sure, not only to make attempts, but to succeed, in an eminent degree, in poetry, since almost the rudest nations have essays of the kind. They, however, have not even any oral traditionary tales, either in verse or in prose ; nor do they seem to have the least taste for hearing such repeated. They are no singers, not even to their own children ; yet are they so far from being deficient in either ear or taste for music, that a very great many of the men are performers on the violin. This art, however, they only pursue as a calling, which may be followed without forsaking their itinerant life or rural station. The fiddle is never heard in their tents for the gratification of their family. It is, with them, an instrument of profit, not of amusement.

There is, too, a peculiar sedateness and seriousness in their manners and conversation. They are very rarely heard talking lightly, or laughing, among

each other : yet, I apprehend, they think but little
on religious subjects, nor are they influenced, it
appears, in general, by religious motives.   They
would, perhaps, rather avoid talking at all respecting it, as they never introduce it ; nor are they, I
apprehend, in the habit of praying ; but when ques-
tioned respecting religion, they never speak lightly
or irreverently of it ; nor are they addicted to common swearing ; but as regards religion, they seem
influenced, as in most other things, by a desire to remain unmolested, and to avoid giving offence : they,
therefore, profess to accord with the views of the
people among whom they are "*scattered.*"   Bap-
tism appears to be the only religious act, respecting
which they are in any degree really anxious.   I
believe that they in general wish to have that cere-
mony performed.   As to marriages, if they can
have them performed in a church, they would, in
most instances, prefer it ; but if want of money, or
other circumstances, seem to stand in the way, they
scruple not, as before observed, to pledge their
faith, and " take each other's word ;" such marriages being held inviolable amongst them.   If left
to themselves, I believe that they very rarely attend
divine service, even when encamped near a church.
Like their fellow offenders and sufferers, the Jews,
their eyes appear to be blinded, and their hearts
hardened, for their transgressions, till God's time
shall come for their "conversion and healing."   In
both instances, the *heart* seems totally unmoved by
any feelings of affection, or desire of communion
with God.   This circumstance, in either people,

would be remarkable ; but as applying to *both*, it is most extraordinary. Regular as the Jews may often be in their attendance on public worship, it seems clearly with them only a prescribed cere- mony, with which the *heart* has nothing to do.

All the circumstances which have been here re- lated as regards the Gypsies, seem to me most clearly to prove them to be, as before said, a people ordained by the Divine decree to be "scattered among the nations, and dispersed in all countries," in the *open fields* thereof, so to remain unchanged during a certain period, said, in the language of prophecy, to be forty years. All their singular habits, their propensities, their feelings, as here stated, are such as to fit them for, and continue them in such a state. Nay, the proceedings of the rulers of the numerous nations and countries in which they have been "dispersed and scattered" for so many ages, seems to have been overruled to contribute to their so remaining, though many of those proceedings were expressly designed to ex- tirpate them. There is scarcely a country in Europe in which severe edicts have not been passed against the Gypsies, decreeing their punishment and expulsion. In no one instance, however, have they succeeded. In England many penal laws were enacted against them, and very great numbers were executed for no other crime but being Gypsies. At one Suffolk assize, no less than thirteen of these poor wretches were executed together, legally con- victed of being born of Gypsy parents. By these means, however, the race was not expelled, though many of them were driven for a time to seek a more secure asylum in the Peak of Derbyshire, and other unfrequented parts of the country. No sooner, however, were the persecutions abated, than they resumed their former circuits.

On any supposition but that of a miraculous interdiction, restraining the Gypsies from leaving, till the appointed time, the "open fields" of any of the "nations through which they are scattered," or any one of the "countries in which they are dispersed," it is impossible to account for such a pertinacious adherence, at the risk of liberty and life, to habits which to almost all other people would appear appalling. They were not required even by their oppressors to do any thing respecting which they had any conscientious scruples, or to which they could have any reasonable strong objections, but only to live and labour as others did. It seems, however, that they were restrained from so doing by an unseen Almighty power, and, therefore, no compulsion has been able to counteract the decree of Omnipotence.

SUPPLEMENT.

"Let no man, therefore, despise him, but conduct him
forth in peace, that he may come unto me, for I look
for him with the brethren."—1 Cor. xvi., 11.

In order duly to appreciate the marvellousness
of the circumstances under which the Gypsies are
represented to have been, when the first accounts
of them—of which we know—were written, it will
be necessary to cast our eyes over the history of
nations from the deluge, for the purpose of seeing,
if an expelled people have ever, in any other instance, been so found.

It was just before the invention of printing, i. e.
from 1400 to 1440, that accounts were written which
have reached us of their being then in almost every
country of Europe, and many parts of Asia. In
general they were not wandering in hordes, from
country to country, but stationary in almost every
one of them. Not large colonies of them in some
one place, but dispersed in each nation, in clans, or
families ; seldom more than from ten to thirty together. Within that period there are accounts of
their being in France, Spain, Portugal, Italy, Eng-

K

land, Holland, Germany, Poland, Hungary, Switzer-
land, Bohemia, Turkey, Livonia, Lithuania, Denmark, Norway, Sweden, Transylvania, Wallachia,
Moldavia, and many other countries, in all dispersed
in the same manner, at one and the same time. All
the accounts agree in stating them as being strangers,
coming from no one knew whither, or by what
means. Yet in all instances it would appear, that
they could speak the language of the country in
which they were found, not only making themselves
understood, but professing to tell fortunes. From
all the accounts it appears, I think, that, on the
whole, they were then as numerous as they are now.
In Spain they have been calculated to exceed forty
thousand ; in Great Britain, thirty thousand ; in
Hungary, fifty thousand ; in Moldavia, Wallachia,
the Sclavonian Mountains, and very many other
countries, quite as numerous.

Now then, how are we to account for such a multitude of strangers being *so* found, in almost every
country of the then known world ?

Whenever the people of any country, from any
cause, leave that country in great numbers together,
they will, like all other great bodies, cease to move
as soon as the impetus which acts upon them ceases
to operate. If that impetus be oppressive tyranny,
the security of the nearest mountain heights and
recesses, or the first place beyond the boundary of
the tyrant's power, will be sought and confided in.
If the impetus arise from famine, the nearest countries that afford them subsistence will stop their
progress. If the impetus be the effects of ambition,

a desire of farther possessions, or the gratification of revenge, the objects being obtained, the efforts will cease. In the first instance, the emigrating people will, in all probability, carry with them, and retain their ancient habits, laws, and customs, modified only so far as varying circumstances may require. In the second, the people wandering in search of subsistence, must disperse themselves for that purpose, conforming to the habits, laws, and customs, of those among whom they may succeed in obtaining it, and eventually becoming incorporated and amalgamated with them. In the third instance, the effects must depend upon circumstances. They may compel the conquered people to conform to *their* laws and customs ; they may adopt, in a great measure, those of the conquered country and people, or, as is most likely to be the case, an admixture of both will be adopted. At all events in the end, all distinction is almost certain to be lost. Instances of all these cases may be found in abundance in the history of the world ; but I am not aware of any one which—left to the natural course of events—may not be included in one or other of them.

Of all the extirpated nations of antiquity, I do not know of one (not especially decreed by prophesy to preservation) the people of which have remained a distinct race, among the inhabitants of many other countries, in the which they have been dispersed. In fact, there are only two such instances known of in the world ! the Jews and the Gypsies. As to the Jews, scarcely any one now doubts that they are to this time, preserved by the peculiar appointment (as declared by the Prophets) of Divine Providence. Let us see, then, if it be possible to conceive that the other people, the Gypsies, could, but by the especial appointment of God, have been brought into such a situation as they were first found in, or have been preserved in it, in the manner that they have been.

It is now more than four hundred years that the Gypsies have been known, from authentic accounts, to have been inhabiting almost every country in Europe. In all they were evidently the same people. In all they were considered as being strangers from some very distant country. None of the accounts attempt to assign either the cause of their coming, the way in which they first came, or the period when they, or their forefathers, left their native land. These accounts of them became more numerous soon after the art of printing became known and practised. From all of them it would appear, that these strangers were then able to converse with the natives of the several countries in which they then resided. They therefore could not be just arrived in them. Though the Gypsies universally asserted that they were from Egypt, it does not appear that any of them could give any account of that country, or of the cause, the time, or the manner of their leaving it. All these circumstances tend to prove that they were the descendants of those who had left it ages before. From almost every country they are described as being Fortune-tellers, a circumstance in itself exceedingly remarkable as applying to a people so

numerous and so widely dispersed. It certainly
evinces a great degree of sagacity, and a long
knowledge of the people and their language with
whom they sojourned. They are said to have had
their ears bored and ornamented with rings, many of
them having cups and other articles of silver in their
possession. In various instances, the hordes or families were under leaders, who appeared on horseback,
styled Dukes, Counts, and Lords of Lesser Egypt.
In every country, they appear from the first as
living in separate hordes, tribes, or families, dispersed, generally, in the unoccupied parts. In no
country, in no instance, are they described as
soliciting employment, or as seeking to obtain a
livelihood, either as domestic servants, as culti-
vators of the soil, in the navy, in the army, as
mechanics, or, in short, in any capacity which
distressed strangers would certainly both willingly
and gladly have done. They appeared, on the
contrary, as little independent clans, denizens of
the open wilds, seemingly molesting no one, and
anxious only to remain themselves unmolested.
Hence, probably, it was that they obtained so little
notice. When they came in contact with the inhabitants of the countries in which they resided,
it was most likely in the pursuit of their itinerant
habits of periodically removing from one part of
the country to another, this practice being general
with them all.

Now let any man of common sense imagine
eight hundred thousand or a million people, of any
nation, expelled by any cause, from their native

country, can he entertain a doubt but that such a
poor, distressed multitude would disperse in all
directions, and that all those who did not perish
in the attempt, would endeavour to obtain settle-
ments, wherever, howsoever, and as soon as ever
they could?   He might imagine, perhaps, though
certainly very improbably, that a very few of
them might, by some means or other, find their
way through unknown lands, stormy seas, and over
almost impassable mountains, from Hindostan or
Egypt, to England, France, or Spain—but what
then?   Why then, they would most certainly be
ready to embrace any opportunity of obtaining a
livelihood among the people of the land in which
they had arrived.   But this can only be an imagi-
nary case?   No one can believe that, humanly
speaking, such an instance even to *twenty* such
people could really have occurred.   But what is
the incontrovertible fact, as relates to the Gypsies?
Why, that not only *twenty* of such people were
actually found to have arrived in both *France* and
Spain, but *others also*, at the same time, in twenty
other countries in the same quarter of the globe.
Nay, not only one twenty of such arrived in each
of those countries, but, perhaps, from a hundred
to five hundred such hordes or clans of them, in
every one of those countries.

The foregoing circumstances are, indeed, wonderful, but they are only the beginning of the
wonders attaching to the astonishing event. These
people were not only of habits differing from those
of the people among whom they were found, but

also, in many respects, from those of all the people that then were known, or ever had been known to exist on the face of the earth. Singular too, as these habits were, they were found to be universally the same throughout the almost innumerable hordes of them then scattered among all the nations of the "uncircumcised;" as if they had dropped, in such hordes, from the heavens above, no one seeming to know, (not even themselves) how or when they came there. More wonderful still, though the innumerable scattered hordes of these singular and unprivileged strangers have now been known to have existed, in all these countries during four hundred years, not one single horde has ever either adopted the habits and customs of its fostering country, nor even forsaken, in any important point, the habits and the customs of their first known forefathers. The whole people in all countries, without having had any communication together during the whole of the four centuries, have all remained in this singular state, unchanged in any respect.

From the first of their being known to the present time, these strangers have been admitted to be the most sagacious people ever known as occupying a station so low in society, as the one which they have all invariably retained throughout. It cannot then have been for want of capacity that they have not adopted the more civilized and respectable manners of those about them.

There have been, and there still are, nations, or people, residing constantly in tents, and removing frequently from place to place. But these are continuing the habits of their forefathers from age to

age, in countries, and under circumstances, favourable to such a practice, and where the whole community follow the same.   They have possessions
of flocks and herds, camels, and riches of various
kinds.   They live not strangers among those that
despise them, and whose superior enjoyments and
attainments are continually tempting them to forsake their own simple and abstemious habits.   The
Gypsies on the contrary, have universally adopted,
and continue to persevere in, a mode of living totally unfitted for many of the countries, and climes,
in which they exist; a mode which it has never
been imagined—come from where they may—to
have been that of their forefathers; a mode too,
totally before unknown in practice, in all the countries in which they reside.   Though they see all
around them toiling, and striving, in every way, to
acquire, and lay up riches; they never, in any instance, seem actuated by the same desire to attain
the same object.   The obtaining from day to day,
their daily bread, seems to be about the utmost that
any of them aspire to; otherwise, in the course of
four hundred years, some one, out of eight hundred
thousand, (during that period, ten millions) of a
sagacious people, dispersed throughout Europe,
would have acquired at least, somewhat of lands,
and houses, to have left to their children; but no
one such instance, I believe, is on record.   They
have never been known to gather into barns, and
yet, some way or other, their Heavenly Father,
constantly feedeth them.   It seems as if He had
decreed them this, and denied them more.

While all other people may be described by

what they possess, the Gypsies may be most strikingly designated, and distinguished from all other
people, by here stating what they do *not* possess ;
They have no religion, i. e. no religion peculiar, or
common to them as a people. They have no places
of worship, they have no priests, or professed
teachers—no mode of worship. They have no
idols, no images, or outward symbols, no superstitious observances, no places of sepulchre. They
have no country. In all places where they reside,
they are aliens. They have no pedigrees, no ancestors of whose exploits they are proud : no love
of fame, no desire to live in the remembrance of
those who may descend from, and succeed them.
They have neither manuscript nor printed books
in their language—with scarcely an exception—
they can neither write nor read. They are no de-
lineators. They have no oral tales, or poems.
They are neither dancers, singers, nor whistlers.
They possess no arms of any kind, either offensive
or defensive. They are no robbers nor midnight
plunderers. If any instances have occurred, they
have been so rare, as only to form a striking exception. And, what is very remarkable, situated
as they are, they are very rarely *poachers*, though
they must frequently be greatly tempted to become
such.

To whom does all the foregoing combinations of
extraordinary negative qualities pertain ? If they
had been possessed by some little horde of strangers, residing for a few months, or years, in any
neighbourhood, such would have been thought

a very extraordinary people. But in this instance,
they appertain, invariably, to perhaps more than
ten thousand such hordes, dispersed throughout
the whole of Europe, and a great part of Asia,
(having in general, no communication with each
other,) and to no one else in the whole world.
Nor is all this a temporary coincidence only — on
the contrary, their peculiarities appear to have attached to them all, from the very first accounts of
that singular people.

All the afore-mentioned wonderful peculiarities,
mark the Gypsies for a people so dispersed, so disposed, and so preserved, by an Omnipotent Being,
either for past transgression, for future designs, or
for both. They appear to me like a people thus
dispersed and long preserved, throughout almost
the whole civilized world, to attract its attention,
in order to display to it, hereafter, some signal instance of Almighty Power. They seem to me
thus kept apart, and totally unconnected with the
people among whom they reside, to be ready at a
moment's call. They have no possessions—no at-
tachments—no connections—no patriotism to de-
tain them. They have no political, no religious,
no long established prejudices to overcome. They
have no luxurious habits, no superstitious observances, no forms or ceremonies to impede them on
their way. On the contrary, they are a bold, a
hardy, a sagacious, a persevering race. Accustomed to constant travelling, and to the greatest
privations, they would neither shrink from danger,

nor faint under difficulties... At an hour's notice, every one of the eight hundred thousand (supposing that to be the number of them,) would be ready to commence their march. For the young, the aged, and infirm, they are always provided with conveyances. Starting from such numerous, and distant stations, their progress, till they began to concentrate, would scarcely be found to be an inconvenience.

Looking then, at this astonishing people, only as we know them to exist at this time, and as we know that they have existed for four hundred years ; setting prophecy apart, we cannot, I think, but come to the conclusion, that such an anomaly in the history of the human race, does not exist, nor has so long existed, but for some purpose out of the usual course of Divine Providence. God never acts in vain, nor ever creates an instrument, that hath not a work to perform. It cannot then be, but that this extraordinary people are reserved in the manner, and the state, that they are, for a work as extraordinary as they themselves are. What that work is to be, was, I think, clearly foretold more than two thousand years ago, by the prophets of the Lord, in language too sublimely impressive, too strikingly forcible, and too clear and explicit, to be either disregarded or misunderstood, excepting by the inattentive, or the wilfully blind and deaf. This subject has been treated at considerable length in a late publication, entitled "PARALLEL MIRACLES," endeavouring to prove, that according

to prophesies, the Gypsies are the descendants of
the ancient Egyptians, and that they are hereafter
to be reassembled in their own country, and to be
brought under a *Saviour* and a *Great One*, to
know the Lord.

APPENDIX.

A GYPSY FAMILY.

Since this work went to press, I was informed that, there was a public-house in the town kept by Gypsies. As this was an uncommon circumstance, and as I wished to obtain more information respecting that people, I lost no time in calling at the house, and enquiring for the landlord. I was shown into a little parlour, and after a while he came to me. His appearance was not prepossessing. He seemed suspicious and embarrassed. He left the door open and sat down by the side of it. After informing him, who I was—I told him that I had taken the liberty of calling, really wishing to serve him, to ask him a few questions, which, I nevertheless, did not wish him to answer, if not quite agreeable. I said, that during some years I had been much interested respecting the *Gypsies*—without speaking a word, he here arose, and abruptly left the room. Not knowing the reason, and supposing that he might be gone for something, or for some one, I sat a considerable time waiting.

At length I rang the bell, when the wife came in. I told her that I had called to have some conversation, which I thought might be of service, with her husband, but that he had left me, and I did not know whether he was returning or not. She said that she believed that he was gone out, but asked if she could not give me the information that I wanted? She was a quick, lively, rather good looking little woman, evidently only half cast, but with bright dark Gypsy eyes. She sat down, and I told her that I had some years ago, written a book about the Gypsies, and that I was then going to print another. Her attention was now roused, and she seemed pleased. I had been told that they had a daughter about fourteen, and that the father had asserted that if she married to please him, she should have half a peck of sovereigns. This young lady now came in. If I had seen her any where accidentally, I should have conceived that she was a young *Jewess*. It has long struck me that in the countenances of those who are young and handsome among that people, whether male or female, there is a look of somewhat rather approaching to superhuman. A little of this I thought perceptible in this young half Gypsy. She remained listening, and greatly interested in the conversation.

I told them about Clara's coming to live with us and the way in which she had behaved herself. I asked the mother if she knew anything about the Earnes—her eyes sparkled, while, with her characteristic quickness, she exclaimed " Oh yes ! the Earnes

485

rank the first among the Gypsies—it is well known that they are directly descended from *King Pharoah!*" I however found that she conceived that Pharoah was a King of England, for on asking her if the Gypsies were not originally from Egypt, she said, no such thing. She assured me that the Gypsies were the original inhabitants of *England*, there having been none in it before them. She said that she had not seen any of the Earnes for a long time.

I then took out of my pocket the proof sheet, containing the list of words in the Gypsy language as repeated by Clara, and told her what were the contents. "What!" she cried, "is there a book printed with our *gibberish* in it?" I told her yes. I read some of the words, to which, with a smile and great quickness, she gave the English. I then asked what were the Gypsy names to many of the English words, which she generally gave the same as Clara had given. In some instances she gave a different one, but on my saying what Clara had given, she said, "Yes, that is it too; there are two names." Some few she did not know.

As there were people drinking in the house, and she was wanted to wait on them, I did not stop any longer, but left a part of the book, as she said that her husband could read. There was an appearance of great discomfort throughout: they all (there were four children) seemed like beings out of their natural element. I was, however, glad to have the accuracy of Clara's information confirmed; while the behaviour of the man strongly evinced that jealous suspicion of all inquiries into their peculiar circumstances, which is very general among them, strongly indicating their designation to remain a distinct people.

I must request my readers now, at the conclusion, to recollect the observations made in the commencement of this work, viz. that the great object of it was to enforce what I conceived to be a most important *truth*, i. e. that the Gypsies are the descendants of the ancient Egyptians, dispersed among all nations for their sins during many ages, and finally to be restored to the land of their forefathers, as foretold by the three great prophets of Israel. That all circumstances relating to their conduct during the time of their dispersion, are of very minor importance, no way affecting the great truth in question, though, abstractedly considered, they are of themselves most intensely interesting. Different writers on the subject have, from various causes, been induced to represent them differently. This must inevitably be the case, as relates to the moral conduct of such a people; but whatever that may have been, it in no degree affects the truth that has been here attempted to be established; a truth, the importance of which no one that I am acquainted with, brought before the public during the last eighteen hundred years, by any means equals. This assertion, taking the subject in all its bearings, will, I conceive, scarcely be denied.

Are you then prepared, it may be asked, to state when these predicted occurrences may be expected to take place? Certainly not! Times and seasons are known to God alone. *He* is not slack concerning his promises ; but, it must be remembered, that with Him a thousand years are but as one day. There are, however, at this time strong intimations that the end of all predicted things is drawing nigh, a circumstance which must be preceded by the coming in of the Gentile world. More progress has been made towards the promotion of that object during the last half century, than probably, during the preceding thousand years. This has not been solely the effect of the exertions of the Christian world ; but the way, as it seems to me, had been gradually prepared for them by the hand of Almighty Power, in the extension of decrepitude and enfeebled dotage, over all the old idolatrous superstitions of the world.

Perhaps I cannot enforce this surmise better than by the following short and impressive extracts from " Saturday Evening," a publication replete with the strongly expressed sentiments of a deeply reflecting mind, by the Author of the " Natural History of Enthusiasm :"—

" Nothing more remarkably distinguishes the religious state of mankind in our own times, as compared with any other eras, concerning which history enables us at all to form an opinion, than the air of DOTAGE which belongs, *without exception*, to every one of the leading superstitions of the nations. There have been times when, if some were on their wane, others were in full vigour, or just starting forth from their cradle with a giant strength. If we track the course of time during the lapse of four-and-

twenty centuries, we shall find this to have been the
case in each period.   In each there was, in some
quarter within the circle of historic light, or its
penumbra, one or more forms of religious error
which very firmly grasped the minds of the nations
that were its victims.

    *   *   *   *

  " But it seems now as if there were neither
courage nor concert in the halls of aërial government.   Not only is every extant form of error ancient—most of them immemorially so ; but every
form is *imbecile,* as well as old. Or if we would seek
a phrase that should at once describe the present
condition of false religion, universally, we find it
in the expression already quoted— *The errors of
mankind are now ' antiquated, and in their dotage,'*
—Dare we so far penetrate futurity as to add—
' They are ready to vanish away ?'

    *   *   *   *

  " The heroic savage who stalks through the wilderness of America, and the pallid Mongul, and the
feverish Tartar, of central Asia, and the luxurious
islander of the Southern and Pacific Ocean, are
men upon whose visage, in whose customs, and in
whose belief, we read the characters of a distant
age :—they all may boast *an ancestry,* and they
possess a memorial. They are not the mere pro-
geny of the desert, born of oblivion, and destined to
oblivion ; but the descendants of MEN ; and the
races they belong to are the wrecks of primitive
empires.   A personage of princely birth and educa-
tion has wandered far from his patrimony, has fallen

from his rank, has endured many degradations, has
forgotten his rights : nevertheless there is an in-
alienable greatness about him ; and even the trum-
pery of the ornaments he wears contains proof of
his noble lineage. Like every thing else that distinguishes these fallen and impoverished families,
their religion is—a RELIC. And it is a relic, faded
in colours, and decayed. If the history of the sub-
jugation of the empires of Mexico and Peru, and if
that of the Tartar conquests of the midle ages, and
if the imperfect notices of the ancient Scythian nations, preserved by the Greek writers, may be taken
as affording the means of a comparison between the
present and the past religious condition of those
classes of the human family of which we are speaking, it is quite manifest that the dimness, and the
incertitude, and the terrors of extreme age have
come upon all their superstitions. The force of the
fanaticism they once engendered is spent. The
demon is less the object of terror, is less often and
less largely propitiated with blood ;—the priest is
less a prince than he was, and more a mercenary.
Yes, and symptoms have appeared, even in this class
—of incredulity and reason. No phrase better describes these now fading errors, than that already
quoted—they are all ' superannuated and decayed
with age.'

    *   *   *   *

  " The Mahometan *empire* is decrepit ; Mahometan *faith* is decrepit : and both are so by confession
of the parties. In matters both civil and religious,
those days are come upon this superstition in which

—'The *sun* and the *moon*, and the stars, are darkened;' nor do 'the clouds (of refreshment) return after the rain.—And the keepers of the house tremble; and the strong bow themselves; and the grinders (the powers of mechanic art and trade) cease, because they are few.   And they that look out at the windows (the learned class) are darkened. And the doors are shut in the streets (by jealousy and depopulation) and the wakefulness of conscious danger is upon it; and the daughters of music (revelry) are brought low; and fears are in the way; and desire faileth.'

    *   *   *   *

" Is it indeed a gratuitous assumption, advanced only to give completeness to an argument, when we say—That the religion of the Prophet is now in its stage of extreme decrepitude ?

    *   *   *   *

" Least of all, then, should any calling themselves Christians, now feel, and speak, and act, as if they abhorred advancement; or as if decay and slumber were far less dreaded by them, than change, even of the happiest sort.

    *   *   *   *

" Let the fond admirer of his own Church, whatever may be its pretensions, assure himself, that the conversion of Asia, and Africa, and Europe, and America, will so raise the temperature—spiritual and moral, of the world's atmosphere, as must dissolve, to its very elements, every community now calling itself a Church.   All principles shall then invest themselves in new power, all notions of good and evil be recast, all forms and constitutions be new modelled. We shall indeed believe the same things as now; but in another manner: we shall practice the same virtues, but at a different rate, with firmer motives, and under the guidance of an extended exposition of every precept.

"Instead therefore of cherishing a blind attachment to phrases, modes, usages, opinions, which are separable from the substance of religion, wise and docile spirits, though they may not hope fully to anticipate 'in imagination' changes that are to be effected, will at least preserve with care a state of feeling, such as shall prove the best preparative for joining in with whatever may attend the expected "times of refreshment."

Perhaps no people, not really Christians, are better prepared to chime in with such a general amalgamation of the human race than the Gypsies are. They, of all others, will have the least of error to *unlearn*; and, after all, *that* is generally the most difficult, as well as the first step towards acquiring a knowledge of the truth. By having been kept, as predicted to themselves, despised in the *open fields*, without *Idols*, God seems to have retained them constantly ready to obey that call to a knowledge of the truth as it is in Christ Jesus, which I can have little or no doubt is finally to be extended to them in the land of their forefathers.

They, with the Jews, (both predicted) are the only instances in the history of the world of any people thrown at once into a state in which they were to remain for long periods unaltered, and in which they, as I conceive, *have* remained so unaltered, during almost two thousand years. All others have had their feeble infancy, vigorous youth, powerful manhood, and decrepit old age ; and this, not only as relates to their political existence, but also as respects their various systems of religion. Christianity alone has stopped short of the last state ; but even with her, change and apparent incertitude has been perpetual. We have, indeed, scriptural authority, as well as that of experience, for asserting that all things in this world are constantly changing. The Jews and the Gypsies appear, however, to have been, during nearly two thousand years, extraordinary exceptions to this general rule ; yet were they both, before their present states were decreed, as much subjected to change as any other people.

It is highly remarkable too, that the respective states into which the two people before mentioned, were decreed by the Divine fiat, and in which they still remain, were as different as could well be conceived, from those which they had formerly occupied. God, however, by His prophets (as moved by the Holy Ghost), decreed them their respective extraordinary conditions, in which to remain unaltered till it should please Him to recall them to their forfeited patrimony. They are both of them now awaiting that call, unable, and indeed, indisposed, to extricate themselves from their decreed long thraldom. During nearly two thousand years, have they each respectively thus remained unchanged. That state has known no infancy, no

youth, no manhood, no old age. There has been
no growing in strength, nor has there been any decay. The decreed blindness rests upon them both,
and will so rest, till God, in his own good and predicted time, shall withdraw the bandage from their
eyes. All this must have declared a miraculous
interference, had nothing still more astonishing
accompanied it, but these two people, thus never
changing, have not been, are not, compacted together in their respective countries, but are each of
them scattered, almost singly, among nearly all
people, nations, and languages, in the civilized
world, the one people, (as before stated,) in the cities
and populous towns, and the other in the wildernesses and open fields. Neither people, either have,
have had, nor can have, any system of government,
yet do they both act—throughout the whole of each
dispersed race, with more of unanimous accordance
than any other people, equally numerous, on the
face of the earth. Since their dispersion, there
has been no change, neither shadow of turning.
As God sent them forth, attesters of His power in
the cities and fields of all the earth, so do they remain, and so will they be found, when the awful
summons for their return to their respective father-
lands shall reach their ears.

THE END.

SHEFFIELD : WHITAKER AND CO. PRINTERS.

85 Their religious mission and duty as damned outcasts to earn their forgiveness?
129 Without going into modern Israel and all that. ✓
153 Deep swarthy Egyptian clasic comelexion.
169 Only the violin for music, no poetry or singing.

Lightning Source UK Ltd.
Milton Keynes UK
UKOW07f1822020615

252771UK00004B/238/P